TRULY OF THE FEW

The Polish Air Force in
the Defence of Britain

Dr Penny Starns

SABRESTORM

This book is dedicated to members of the Polish Air Force who lost their lives during the Second World War.

Designed and typeset by Philip Clucas MSIAD

British Library Cataloguing in Publication Data

A catalogue record for this book is available from the British Library

Published by Sabrestorm Publishing, The Olive Branch, Caen Hill, Devizes, Wiltshire SN10 1RB

Website: www.sabrestorm.com
Email: books@sabrestorm.com

ISBN 978-1-78122-019-1

Contents

Foreword
by Richard Kornicki

It is often said that in 1940 Britain fought alone. But although most of Europe was occupied by German forces, there was one country which, although occupied, never surrendered, never signed an armistice, and never gave up the fight. That country was Poland. Its legal Government continued in exile; it kept the commitments of its Treaty with Britain; and Polish armed forces fought by land, sea and air until the end of the war.

Penny Starns here tells the story of the Polish Air Force in the West for the general reader. Her account is brought to life with the words of some of the 20,000 men and women who served in the Polish Air Force. While readers may be aware of the outstanding contribution of Polish pilots to the Battle of Britain, as this book demonstrates, the same commitment was shown by bomber squadrons and by the ground crews.

Polish airmen were determined to fight on after the fall of Poland. They reached Britain by any route they could find, avoiding capture, internment or death. But at the end of the war, there was no going home for most of them. They had fought for Poland with utter commitment; they had shown unwavering fidelity to the Allied cause; they had made a crucial contribution during the crisis of the Battle of Britain: and in return they saw Poland handed over to the same Stalin who had invaded it in 1939.

Some emigrated to America or the Commonwealth; most stayed in Britain and made a new life for themselves. They and their descendants form the oldest part of the large community of Poles for whom Britain is now home. The achievements of the Polish Air Force, flying alongside the Royal Air Force, constitute a common heritage and should be a common source of pride for Britons and Poles alike. The author is to be congratulated on making their story so accessible as we mark the 80th anniversary of the Battle of Britain.

Above: Richard Kornicki pictured with his father Franciszek Kornicki and the Spitfire (serial-BM597) flown by Franciszek in 317 Squadron..

Speaking in Warsaw in old age, my late father, Generał Brygady Franciszek Kornicki, the last surviving Polish squadron commander, said: "Poland is something that really matters. It is the duty of every citizen to care for her, to serve her, and if necessary, to defend her." This book shows what that meant for his generation.

Richard Kornicki CBE DL
Chairman, Polish Air Force Memorial Committee

SKRZYDŁA
Wiadomości ze Świata
PISMO ŻOŁNIERZY POLSKICH SIŁ POW

"WINGS" —
ODICAL OF THE
SH AIR FORCE

Nr 12 389   15-30 CZERWCA 1942 r.   C.

Introduction

*'In the desperate days of 1940 we fighter pilots were proud
to include in our number Polish airmen who in their own
squadrons, and as individuals in British squadrons did so
much to strengthen and stiffen the depleted ranks of Fighter
Command—as fighter pilots they were second to none.
Great aviators; great comrades; truly of the Few.'
(Air Commodore A.C. Deere D.S.O. O.B.E. D.F.C)*

This book documents the crucial role played by the Polish Air Force (PAF) in defending Britain during the Second World War. Following the German invasion of their native land on 1st September 1939 and its subsequent occupation by German and Russian forces, intrepid, experienced Polish pilots made their way across Europe; determined to fight their enemies from the 'island of last hope.' Their journeys were long and perilous. Some were captured and interned along the way, others arrived at their destinations via incredibly circuitous routes. Those who successfully reached the safety of British shores were already battle hardened, having fought against German oppression in their homeland and in France. They possessed a steely, single-minded approach to war, and were fully committed to fighting their aggressors by any means possible.

Following the fall of France in June 1940 Britain, its Empire and its only Ally, Poland, stood alone against the threat of German expansion. Buoyed by the success of their Blitzkrieg attacks across Europe and the rapid capitulation of France, Hitler and the German high command formulated plans to invade Britain. However, they were unable to implement a lightning speed Blitzkrieg invasion without first crossing the English Channel. Furthermore, 'Operation Sealion,' Hitler's codename for the planned invasion of Britain, needed unequivocal air support from the Luftwaffe to protect the German fleet.

Left: Front cover of a Polish Air Force periodical 1942.

7

Moreover, while the Commander-in-Chief of the Luftwaffe Hermann Goering believed the Nazis to be invincible, German Naval Commanders were less enamoured with invasion plans. The British Royal Navy (RN) had a long established and deserved reputation of being the best naval force in the world, and this supremacy would not easily be subdued by German vessels. The implementation of Operation Sealion therefore, depended almost entirely on the ability of Goering's Luftwaffe to destroy the British Royal Air Force (RAF) and gain control of the air space over Southern England.

With an increasing sense of urgency, the British Prime Minister Winston Churchill acknowledged the inevitability of an imminent aerial battle and the possibility of an invasion. Thus, he gave a stern warning to the British people: 'Upon this battle depends the survival of Christian civilisation. Upon it depends our own British life and the continuity of our institutions and our Empire. The whole fury and might of the enemy must very soon be turned on us now. Hitler knows that he will have to break us in this island or lose the war. If we can stand up to him all Europe may be free, and the life of the world move forward into broad, sunlit uplands. But if we fail, then the whole world including the US, including all that we have known and cared for, will sink into the abyss of a new Dark Age, made more sinister, and perhaps more protracted, by the lights of perverted science. Let us therefore brace ourselves to our duties, and so bear ourselves that, if the British Empire and its Commonwealth last for a thousand years, men will still say, 'This was their Finest Hour.'

The subsequent intense aerial combat between British, Commonwealth and Polish Air Forces, and the Luftwaffe became known as the Battle of Britain and began on 10th July 1940. It was unique in being the first battle in history to be decided by air power alone. In addition to the brave British airmen defending the realm at this crucial time, there were equally brave pilots from Commonwealth countries and those whose countries had already been overrun by German Panzer Divisions and oppressed by the Nazi regime. Among the latter group were courageous Polish pilots who became a vital and integral part of RAF fighter and bomber commands. Along with Polish naval and army servicemen and women these pilots took their instructions from their own superiors, because the Polish Government never officially surrendered territory to their enemies and remained fully operational in exile. Eventually there were fifteen Polish Squadrons, which included engineering expertise, ground crew, intelligence officers, navigators, instructors, Women's Auxiliary Air Force personnel and administrative staff. Polish airmen also served within RAF Squadrons.

Fighting long and hard, with a level of skill, efficiency and tenacity that surprised their British colleagues, Polish pilots achieved outstanding results in aerial combat against the Luftwaffe. From the outset they displayed phenomenal courage, and their ability to engage and shoot down enemy aircraft became legendary. Indeed, the extraordinary Polish 303 Squadron reigned supreme in Fighter Command during the Battle of Britain; and undoubtedly the outcome of this conflict would have been very different without their tremendous support.

With stoical determination, and far from home, Polish pilots continued to put their lives on the line in defence of Britain. PAF Squadron 307 was responsible for defending major cities against incoming German night raiders during the Blitz; and later defended historic cities during the Baedeker raids. Others were given the task of defending coastal areas or, as special duties units, gathering intelligence and assisting underground resistance forces. As the war progressed, Polish airmen were assigned to offensive raids, infiltrating enemy territory and destroying Germany's industrial and rocket bases. They also made a vital contribution to D-Day and the subsequent liberation of Europe. Indeed, from 1940 onwards, members of the PAF wholeheartedly assisted the RAF and staunchly defended Britain throughout the war. An exceptional commitment which was sadly repaid with political treachery in the post war years.

The following text tells the dramatic story of the Polish Air Force through detailed combat reports, logistics of battle strategies, oral history testimonies, operational records and a wide variety of previously unpublished written and visual material. Firmly set within the context of each phase of aerial combat, the book documents the heroic contribution made by the Polish Air Force; not only to one of the most famous battles in history, but also to the ultimate success of long-term Allied objectives.

Sources
Most of the primary source material for this book has been obtained from the National Archives at Kew, London, and the Imperial War Museum Sound and Document Archives at Lambeth, London. This material has been supplemented by Hansard Parliamentary Debates 5th Series (House of Commons), and documents located in local archives.

Chapter 1
Journeys to Britain

Contrary to popular belief British government and military officials began preparing for the Second World War as early as 1922. Civil defence strategies were discussed at some length, and Germany, Italy and Japan were identified as likely future aggressors. Furthermore, because London had been bombed during the First World War these same officials recognised that the main thrust of future attacks would come in the form of aerial bombardment. This was later confirmed by the relentless air raids experienced by Barcelona during the Spanish Civil War. Therefore, although it was difficult for the British government to second guess the actions of potential enemies in the 1920s and early 1930s it was considered prudent to prepare for the worst-case scenario.

The rise of fascism in Italy and Germany prompted the formation of a British Defence Requirement Sub Committee (DRC) in November 1933, and increased concerns surrounding the prospect of aerial warfare. Economic constraints, incurred as a result of the previous global conflict, an adherence to international treaty agreements, and a fear of political unrest, had severely limited Britain's rearmament process. However, subsequent reports generated by the DRC from 1934 onwards highlighted an urgent need to resolve defence issues, especially those pertaining to a threat from the air. Thus, Treasury funding for rearmament within the British Royal Air Force (RAF) was prioritised above the needs of the Royal Navy and the Army in order to achieve parity with Germany. By 1938 the RAF had expanded substantially but still lacked adequate numbers of modern fighter and bomber aircraft. Shadow factories were established to increase production and twenty-seven new ordnance works were built. In addition, the appeasement policy, pursued by British Prime Minister Neville Chamberlain, and his French counterpart Edouard Daladier, towards Hitler, bought Britain some desperately needed rearmament time.

Left: Big Ben and the Houses of Parliament behind barbed wire.

Culminating in the signing of the Munich Agreement on the 30th of September 1938, which ceded the Sudetenland to Hitler, appeasement was a controversial issue. Viewed by many as a shameful policy of weakness, the pursuance of a settlement with a dictator intent on achieving Lebensraum for the German people, appears with hindsight to have been ridiculously optimistic, or politically naïve. Some French historians have even gone so far as to suggest that Daladier was forced to follow British policy in this respect. Yet nothing could be further from the truth. Prior to Daladier's election, the previous French Blum government was ousted by the French people for initiating a five-year arms production programme and placing defence concerns above those of social reform. In effect Daladier was elected on an appeasement ticket, and on his return from Munich was welcomed home by over 500,000 people.[1] Crowds in London also gathered to cheer Chamberlain as he famously waved his bit of paper claiming to have achieved 'peace in our time.'

This public display of joy emanated from a collective sense of genuine relief that war had seemingly been avoided. Nevertheless, although Chamberlain and Daladier had hoped to ensure European stability neither of them seriously believed that Hitler would curtail his expansionist aims. Consequently, the pace of British and French rearmament was accelerated in the aftermath of Munich. In March 1939 when Hitler's army marched into Czechoslovakia appeasement was officially dead. In response to this flagrant breach of the Munich Agreement the British government issued a guarantee to Poland. As Chamberlain explained in the House of Commons:

In the event of any action which clearly threatened Polish independence, and which the Polish government accordingly considered it vital to resist with their national forces; His Majesty's Government would feel themselves bound at once to lend the Polish Government all support in their power. They have given the Polish Government an assurance to this effect. I may add that the French Government have authorised me to make it plain that they stand in the same position in this matter as do His Majesty's Government.'[2] Chamberlain reaffirmed British commitment to Poland again on 25th August 1939 with the signing of the Anglo-Polish alliance.

Thus, in response to the German invasion of Poland on 1st September 1939, Britain and France declared war on Germany on the 3rd September 1939. However, they failed to send military aid to help the Polish defend their territory. In British political circles a declaration of war was considered enough to honour the guarantee extended to Poland earlier in the year. Yet nothing could alter the fact that despite lengthy speeches in parliament, and laboriously worded treaties, both Britain and France reneged on their stated promises to offer their ally 'all support in their power.' This political situation did not sit well with British military personnel. Major General Sir Alfred Knox questioned Chamberlain in the House of Commons, asking:

> *'Whether he thinks it will soon be possible for the Allies in the West to undertake such military operations as may relieve pressure on Poland, which is now fighting for its life?'*[3]

Chamberlain replied: *'I could not possibly answer that question.'*[4]

In the days, weeks and months that followed, Sir Alfred Knox's question was never answered.

The Poles were left to their own devices and fought valiantly, first against the Nazi invasion, then against the Russians, who invaded Poland on 17th September. Lech Łaszkiewicz was working at a telephone exchange when the bombing began:

> *It was mainly army barracks and ammunition depots, but high-level bombing. Population was somewhat stunned. Next day I moved East, out to Warsaw. Someone said—now you are in the Air Force—here we go! It was exciting I suppose. We expected at any time that our Air Force would come and deal with enemy aircraft, but they didn't materialise. Hatred of the enemy came later, when I saw what was happening on the roads. Civilians being mowed down by gun fire, even cows were shot. We went through Warsaw and it was general carnage. Places were burning and bridges had been bombed, we kept going east. Then a Major said – "It's all over and it's every man for himself." He had no more orders and he left us.*
>
> *One night we were sleeping in a barn and heard tanks. In the morning we were behind Russian lines. We decide to go back west, back home to see what was happening. We were a motley crew crossing a potato field which seemed to be empty. Halfway across Germans popped up, so we were escorted back. By then it was just my friend and myself, so we decided to be very young, and wanted to go home to mummy so they virtually let us go.*[5]

Lech arrived back home to discover his older brother missing and his community gathered together in forced labour camps. His mother advised him

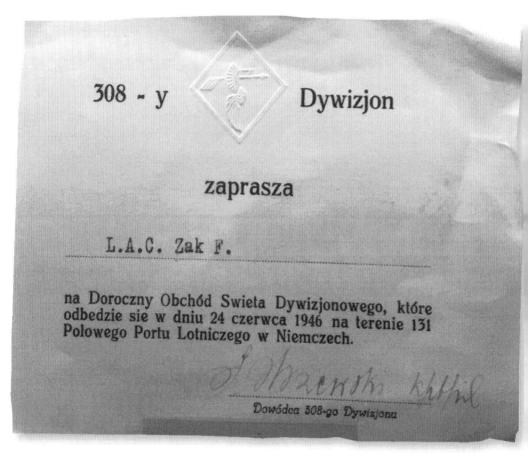

308 - y ⬦ **Dywizjon**

zaprasza

L.A.C. Żak F.

na Doroczny Obchód Święta Dywizjonowego, które odbedzie się w dniu 24 czerwca 1946 na terenie 131 Polowego Portu Lotniczego w Niemczech.

Dowódca 308-go Dywizjonu

Above: Official Polish Papers held at RAF Notholt Museum.

to head west in the hope of reaching France. Along with his friend he set off on a bicycle, aiming to travel through Hungary, Yugoslavia, and Italy to reach France. Both men were caught and sent back to the Hungarian German border twice where they were kept in military barracks. After a few days they were moved to a holding camp for young refugees in Budapest. Some weeks later they managed to get away from the camp and were picked up by a fire chief who hid them amongst his uniformed men until they were safely across the border. He also supplied them with details of a Polish family who would be willing to feed them and offer accommodation. Lech and his brother in arms made their weary way to the Polish Consulate and after a period of ten days were issued with passports. This official identification was deliberately backdated by a year, to give the impression that both Lech and his friend were of non-military age.

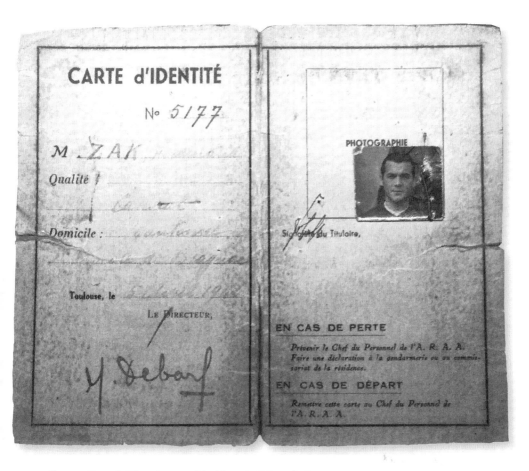

Above: French Identity card held at RAF Northolt Museum.

During their lengthy travels they met a reporter who knew of a Polish family who were resident in Milan. Furnished with their name and address the bedraggled couple journeyed to Italy. As Lech recalled:

When we arrived, it was a very posh place on the main street in Milan. They knew about us and had left information behind for us to go and join them at a restaurant for dinner. We had been on roads for days, sleeping rough, unshaven and in a horrible state. But there we were in a very swish restaurant with private banqueting rooms. They put us up for two or three nights then we went to France to join the French Air Force. I was going to be in the Air Force or else![6]

Thousands of other young Poles also made treacherous journeys to France. On the first day of the invasion Józef Jaworzyn was awoken at 6am and saw Polish aircraft being shot down in a cascade of smoke and flames. By 3pm he had teamed up with his brother and a group of friends to discuss the best plan of action:

> *We were part of the scout movement and had learned to operate anti-aircraft guns. Our scout master was killed by German machine guns, and we lost a teacher in a hand grenade accident. There was a general atmosphere of confusion and disorientation. Masses of people were walking around aimlessly. Radio was silent except for military reports. We could hear fighting getting closer and the blowing up of bridges. Polish army was attacked heavily. They were obliterated. Government employees such as the fire brigade and the police were evacuated from all borders. Whole areas were suddenly devoid of anybody who kept law and order. Train service and roads were blocked by refugees, so it was difficult for the army to get to the front. Only way to go was across mountains to Hungary. We packed our belongings, started up little lanes up mountains and we were joined by many others. They were throwing out equipment, but we picked up clothes to keep us warm later. We picked up grenades and rifles but had to drop some of it because it was too hot to carry everything. We marched for three days and nights, no food except for a bit of ham and water. A spy was shot, and we kicked his body as we walked. There were thousands walking into Hungary. At the border there were emotional scenes of course. We were leaving Poland and dropping anything we could fight with. They (Hungarian border guards) didn't check us but large armaments were given up.* [7]

Józef and his comrades were eventually placed in an industrial complex with no heating, insanitary conditions and minimal food. When the water completely froze over groups of Polish internees managed to steal a radiator unit and a pipe to establish some form of heating. There was considerable unrest as gangs of internees threw bricks at Hungarian soldiers. However, since the latter were armed with machine guns these riots did not last long. A member of the Gestapo was second in command of the camp and encouraged people to return to Poland. People started disappearing in the night, so the list of prisoners dwindled day by day. Younger men were taken to work in factories. It was here that Józef learned of Polish men who had managed to elude captivity and travel west to continue to fight. If he lied about his age it was possible to travel to France by international trains. He, his brother and his band of intrepid friends

Above: Polish insignia displayed at the Polish Museum RAF Northolt.

therefore took two years off their age and became nominal students. Subsequently they reached France via Yugoslavia and Italy. Following instructions from the Polish government in exile Józef's brother joined the Polish army as a communications specialist. Józef meanwhile made his way to Lyon, lying about his age again, because he wanted to become a pilot.

Bolesław Drobiński and two of his friends faced different problems en route to France:

On the 17th September Russia crossed the border into Poland. We went on a train to Sophia in Southern Romania and were housed in barracks normally used for horses. We were disappointed that we couldn't get planes to fly back. People were making false passports and taking photographs. I had toothache so went to main gate, the woman there couldn't speak Polish and I couldn't speak Romanian, but she helped me. I had two names on my passport, so it had to be changed. We were able to get a train to Bucharest on 5th October and a conductor looked at us and said, "where were we going?" With financial help she helped us. Another conductor said it was best not to get off at the platform because Gestapo were at the station. Eventually we arrived at Polish Consulate in Bucharest where an American gave

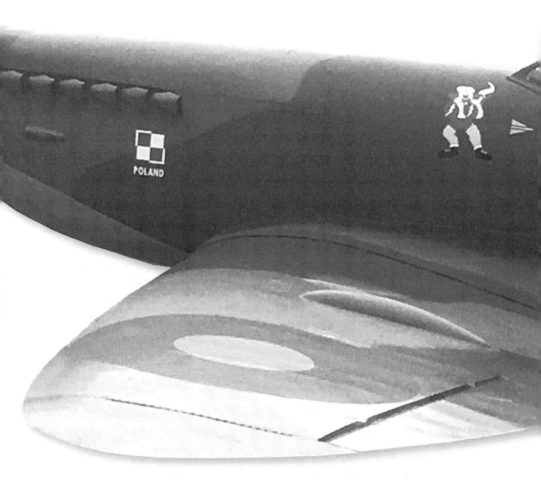

us five dollars each. We were also given train tickets to travel to French/Italian border. The train was full of Italian troops who got drunk. Some people were from Hungary. We were the only three civilians, we were trembling. Then the train stopped because there was a different width of rail. A guard opened our carriage and we followed him to the station. He took us to a room, told us to sit on wooden benches and he locked us in. I had a dagger in my baggage and a lot of photos of our Air Force. I had a revolver, which luckily, I disposed of… probably in the river. An hour passed, then nearly another hour, and he came in and beckoned us to follow him; and he took us to the train station. He said, "I know you are Polish rebels, good luck!" We nearly cried. When we arrived on the French side, we had tea, coffee and canapes. We were lucky on that journey.[8]

Above: *Chequered Polish insignia and artwork on aircraft fuselage.*

By successfully impersonating civilians and using their ingenuity, Lech, Józef, Bolesław and thousands of other Polish military personnel managed to travel across Europe. Upon arrival in France they had mixed feelings. They were eager to fight by any means possible but large swathes of the French population were resentful at being dragged into a war. The Polish Air Force (PAF) was formed in France under instructions from the Polish government in exile, and the main base for existing and aspiring pilots lay just east of Lyon. Existing Polish pilots were experienced, and battle hardened. Even some of the aspiring aviators had a working knowledge of aircraft. Stanisław Andrzej Nawarski, (known as Bob) for example, who had briefly joined his father's infantry unit prior to leaving Poland, made his way to France in November 1939 in the hope of becoming a pilot. He already had considerable experience of flying gliders. On being issued with French identity papers in Lyon he lived alongside French aviators in barracks:

> *The 1939-1940 winter was very cold, but the food was very good. We had ten cigarettes a day and half a litre of wine with our meal. We could have water in a large tin mug. That was my introduction to wine.*

> *Everybody had to do guard duty at different parts of the aerodrome.*
> *We had lectures about aviation law and how controls and engines*
> *worked. We were also learning French, although I already knew French*
> *from secondary school. The aircraft was only for training purposes,*
> *old and delapidated French aircraft. At Christmas I was homesick be-*
> *cause every Christmas before I was with my family. We went to my*
> *grandfather's in the mountains.*
>
> *The French were very disorganised. It was only later, when France*
> *actually collapsed, we realised it was all a charade. Graffiti written on*
> *walls stated: "We must win the war because we are stronger." Nothing*
> *of the b****y sort! Two or three weeks and it is finished, that's how*
> *much stronger they were!*[9]

French military personnel were generally apathetic towards the German threat, and frequently condescending towards the Poles. In some instances, even to the extent of giving brooms and cleaning substances to experienced Polish airmen; along with instructions to clean the French officers' mess. A mixture of collective arrogance combined with a false sense of security undoubtedly pervaded all levels of French society.

Józef Jaworzyn was another Polish pilot disappointed by the lack of French fighting spirit:

> *They were quite antagonistic towards us and said how easily we were*
> *beaten by Germany. They weren't particularly friendly or hospitable;*
> *didn't want to know about our terrible experiences. Poles stood for*
> *something the French did not want to know about.*[10]

Having derided Poles for their failure to prevent the German occupation of their homeland, French armed forces spectacularly collapsed in the face of German aggression a short while later. On 10th May 1940 Germany invaded the Netherlands, Belgium and Luxembourg. Chamberlain resigned as British Prime Minister and was replaced by Winston Churchill. On the 12th May Germans crossed the border into France. Between the 26th May and 4th of June almost 340,000 British and French troops were dramatically evacuated from Dunkirk. On 10th June Italy entered the war on the side of Germany and by 14th June Germany had overrun France and gained control of Paris. The elderly French leader Marshal Petain had little in the way of mental or physical strength with which to fight the Nazis. Therefore, to the utter surprise and dismay of the French, he surrendered France to Germany and formed an official government in Vichy in central France.

Northern France was occupied by German troops while southern France was controlled by Gestapo and Vichy police. The Vichy government collaborated fully with the Nazis and even attempted to recruit Frenchmen into the German armed forces. Once again, the Poles travelled west to continue their fight. This time to Britain, the land they referred to as 'the island of the last hope.' Tadeusz Krzystek, who was a ground crew member of the PAF stated emphatically:

It was our duty to go to a place where we could fight. We could have gone to Sweden or somewhere neutral and wait for the war to be over, but we wanted to attach to units to fight. We wanted to go to the only power still fighting the Germans. Our attitudes towards France and the French were shattered. [11]

Lech Łaszkiewicz and his friends also tried to get to Britain as fast as humanly possible:
Germans advanced very quickly to Paris and we were left on our own again. We tried to get to the railway station to get to England. One thing we observed was there was a lot of Red Cross personnel with stretchers moving in and out from the station and side and back entrances, so we went to the local chemist shop where you could buy these Red

Left: *Polish flag displayed at the Polish Museum RAF Northolt.*

21

Cross bands. We got two arm bands and went back to the station. We called ourselves "service medicale." We just flashed our cards and said, "service medicale" and went straight through and got on the train. We travelled through middle of France and got some orders to report to a military depot and travel to Avignon. Scouting the train, we found it was full of wine and cheese, so we got in cahoots with the driver who sold wine when we stopped to get bread. There was a mixed bunch of around twenty of us and we travelled by freight train but when we arrived in Avignon it was carnage…all gone, nothing for us.' By then we were disgusted by the French. It had been a rather dispiriting experience.[12]

Despite Polish experiences with the French armed forces, thousands of ordinary French people did want to continue the fight against Germany. They were uneasy about Vichy collaboration and fiercely condemned the Nazi occupation. Underground resistance networks were quickly established, and

Above: *The Arandora Star assigned to evacuate allied forces during Operation Aerial.*

many heeded the call of General De Gaulle to join 'Free French' forces. The British meanwhile launched Operation Aerial; a coordinated scheme to evacuate British and allied troops from ports based along the coast of western France. Józef Jaworzyn was one of the men evacuated:

> *There were rumours for some days, then someone said Britain was sending a ship for Polish airmen. We were taken to the harbour, then local fishermen took us to a ship called the Arandora Star. It was solidly packed, no cabin spaces, about 5,000 on board. We got out to the Atlantic quickly to get away from Luftwaffe and U-boats.* [13]

Over one hundred and thirty British and allied liners, ships and small boats were sent to French ports to evacuate civilians as well as troops. Attacked by the Luftwaffe as passengers were being packed into the bowels of ships, some were unable to return to British shores. The Royal Mail Ship Lancastria for instance, was sunk by the Luftwaffe on 17th June at Saint Nazaire. Heavily laden with thousands of troops only two thousand four hundred and seventy-seven passengers and crew were saved. Amid chaotic scenes and enemy bombardment nobody did a head count of those clambering aboard; however, it was estimated the Lancastria was carrying between five and nine thousand people. [14]

Between 15th and 25th June almost two hundred thousand troops were brought to Britain under Operation Aerial. Most of these were British, Polish and Czech personnel. In addition to those rescued from western France there were others who were picked up from the Channel Islands and men, like Bob Nawarski, who had travelled via Gibraltar:

> *We were stuck in Marseilles and didn't know how the war was progressing. We went on to the Spanish border where we thought we could get a boat to Algiers. We were put on a train to Casablanca, then went to the British Consulate and they put us on a coaster to Gibraltar. It took us three or four days to get to England, so we thought we were going to the States.* [15]

Approximately 6,000 thousand Polish airmen had arrived in Britain by the end of July 1940. Most were favourably received. Bob Nawarski recalled his arrival in Liverpool:

> *Everything went from clockwork from there. We couldn't speak any English at all, but we were given a cup of tea and sandwiches. We were*

very impressed with the organization; the fact that there was already a cup of tea waiting and a train seat reserved for us. We were very impressed that somebody actually expected us to come! It was quite funny actually. You thought that if there was a dog fight you knew they would fight you knew they would win the war. Coming to England everything was so organized, it made a great impression. [16]

Józef Jaworzyn was similarly impressed with the British:

We were sent to Blackpool barracks, and it was the first time in ages we could wash, sleep in a clean solid place and wear uniforms. It was a new world. We watched the people with great interest to see what their attitude was to life, to us. We felt far more hopeful. They had more signs of fighting spirit, much more so than in France. But we wondered whether this would be adequate to fight the German brutal machine. [17]

Crowds came out in force to welcome Polish troops and airmen as they arrived in British ports. They cheerfully gave them thumbs up signs and threw cigarettes and flowers at these weary travellers as they disembarked. Polish airmen were then taken to various RAF bases across the country for medical examinations, assessment and training. Furthermore, an Anglo-Polish agreement signed on the 5th August 1940 paved the way for the formation of a fully reconstructed independent Polish Air Force (PAF). Henceforth Polish squadrons and their ground crew played a vital role in the defence of Britain. A role which surpassed all expectations. During July and August numbers 300, 301, 302 and 303 Polish squadrons were established. Subsequently, fifteen Polish Squadrons flew beside the RAF under the latter's command but were ultimately answerable to their own government in exile.

Chapter 2
Organization and Training

Speaking in the House of Commons soon after the fall of France, British Prime Minister Winston Churchill asserted:

> *How ever matters may go in France or with the French government, or with another French government, we in this island and in the British Empire will never lose our sense of comradeship with the French people. If we are called upon to endure what they have suffered we shall emulate their courage, and if final victory rewards our toils, they shall share the gains, aye. And freedom shall be restored to all. We abate nothing of our just demands—the Czechs, Poles, Norwegians, Dutch, Belgians, all who have joined their causes to our own shall be restored. What General Weygand called the Battle of France is over, I expect that the Battle of Britain is about to begin. Upon this battle depends the survival of Christian civilisation.* [1]

Churchill was indeed correct. At this stage, Hitler and his high command were finalising preparations for Operation Sealion—code name for the German invasion of Britain. However, no amount of panzer divisions could rampage through British territory without first crossing the sea. German Naval Commanders however, voiced deep concerns about the daunting prospect of taking on the Royal Navy (RN). They duly informed an overly confident Hermann Goering, Commander in Chief of the Luftwaffe, that German invasion barges would need complete air cover. Operation Sealion therefore, could not be implemented, unless Goering's Luftwaffe was able to destroy the RAF and achieve air supremacy over Southern England. There was also a timescale to consider since weather conditions across the English Channel were bound to deteriorate by the end of September.

Air Chief Marshall Sir Hugh Dowding of the RAF however was already ahead of the game in terms of preparing for a German aerial onslaught. He had laid firm foundations for Fighter Command in 1936 and devised an integrated air defence system. Moreover, despite some questionable planning at the Air Ministry Dowding's system provided an efficient chain of command, which rapidly filtered intelligence information signalling approaching enemy raids, and directed pilots into combat accordingly. In addition to controlling Fighter Command this unified framework incorporated ground defences such as the Observer Corps, radar stations, positioning of barrage balloons, locations of anti-aircraft machinery, and the use of search lights to pick out enemy bombers against the night sky. It also ensured that limited resources were used wisely. Crucially, the process of rapidly interpreting and disseminating large swathes of information relied on a Defence Teleprinter Network (DTN), which efficiently connected Fighter, Bomber, Coastal and Maintenance Commands.

The heart of the DTN consisted of five large switching centres located around the country. Smaller switchboards and teleprinter terminals were spread strategically around the British Isles at military and government establishments. In London and provincial cities, the equipment was located in underground bunkers or heavily reinforced buildings known as Citadels. By the end of 1944 the DTN network had trebled in size.[2]

RAF Group Organisation

Number 10 Group—led by Air-Vice Marshall Sir Christopher, Joseph Quintin Brand K.B.E., D.S.O., M.C., D.F.C., defended South-West England and Wales. Brand whole-heartedly supported Air Chief Marshall Sir Hugh Dowding and Air-Vice Marshal Sir Keith Park during the Big Wing controversy. Number 10 Group also supported number 11 Group when necessary.

Number 11 Group—led by Air-Vice Marshall Sir Keith Rodney Park G.C.B., K.B.E., M.C. & Bar., D.F.C., defended London and South-East England. Park directed operations during the Battle of Britain and later improved the air defence of Egypt and Malta. Park, like Dowding, advocated the rapid deployment of small groups of fighter aircraft to intercept Luftwaffe attacks.

Number 12 Group—led by Air Vice-Marshall Trafford Leigh-Mallory K.C.B., D.S.O., & Bar, defended the Midlands, East Anglia and some sections of Northern England. Leigh-Mallory advocated the Big Wing tactical approach to fighting. This involved joining five Squadrons into a single formation to confront enemy raids. However, this policy resulted in delayed reaction times and was only successful on one occasion.

Number 13—led by Air-Vice Marshall Richard Ernest Saul C.B., D.F.C., defended the remainder of Northern England, Southern Scotland and Northern Ireland.

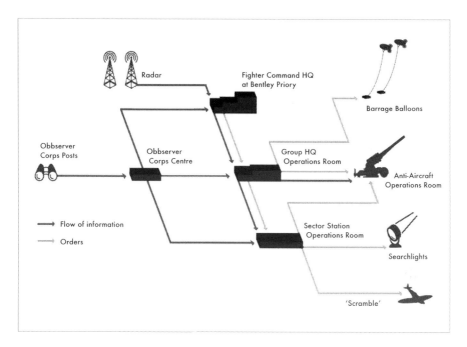

Above: Hugh Dowding's unified air defence framework.

RAF defence of Britain was organized into four distinct groups. Number ten group was responsible for defending South West England and Wales, number eleven group covered London and South East England, number twelve the Midlands, East Anglia and sections of Northern England, and number thirteen the remainder of Northern England, Southern Scotland and Northern Ireland. The groups were subdivided into sectors, each with an operations room, airfields and sector stations. To alert RAF headquarters of incoming German raids a series of range and direction finding (RDF) stations called Chain Home was established along the South East coastline. These faced outwards towards the sea, however, so were unable to track aeroplanes once they were flying inland. To resolve this problem an Observer Corps provided additional information by identifying, tracing, and reporting the course of enemy aircraft to RAF Fighter Command.[3]

Dowding's sophisticated defence structure required highly skilled personnel on the ground. With men required in the fighting forces, sector stations across the RAF employed members of the Women's Auxiliary Air Force (WAAF) to work in a wide variety of roles. Many were trained as operations room plotters, who tracked the strength and course of approaching German raids according to intelligence reports received from Chain Home and Observers. Wooden blocks were colour coded to indicate the time information was acquired. They also displayed other relevant data such as the strength and name of raids. As WAAF members carefully moved these blocks across a huge map table to signal the position of enemy aircraft, arrows were placed behind them to show the direction of attack. A uniquely designed operations room clock assisted this process and ensured that information was constantly updated. Essential to ground controlled interception the clock consisted of five-minute sector teeth, blue, yellow and red triangular sections, with a twenty-four and a twelve-hour dial. Aircraft positions were recorded using the colour of the triangle beneath the minute hand at the exact time of sighting. These positions were then relayed to Fighter Command and sector operations rooms. Thus, initial information was relayed from RDF stations to Fighter Command Headquarters at Bentley Priory, it was then communicated to Group Headquarters who responded with tactical decisions. Group subsequently alerted relevant sector

Above: Members of the Women's Auxiliary Air Force moving coloured blocks across a map table to indicate position of enemy raids.

Above: The uniquely designed Operation Room Clock at the Battle of Britain Bunker.

stations, who were responsible for vectoring Squadrons to intercept the enemy. Each level had its own plotting table covering national, Group and Sector activity respectively.[4]

In the summer of 1940, air defences were firmly in place. However, the RAF was desperately short of experienced pilots and instructors having sustained considerable losses in France. Therefore, despite German propaganda which had belittled the fighting prowess of the PAF, they cautiously welcomed the influx of battle-hardened and aspiring Polish pilots, along with their ground crew. Yet with varying years of flying experience and differing levels of expertise it was something of a challenge to assimilate these newcomers into existing RAF stations. Language barriers compounded this problem.

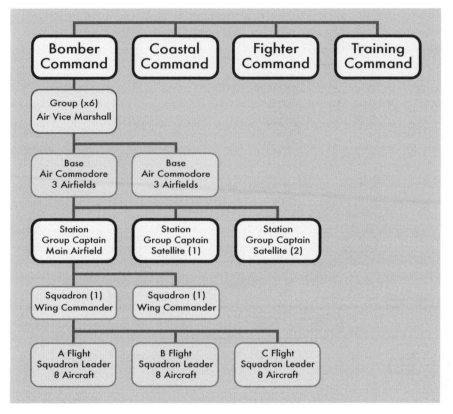

Above: Diagram showing the organisation of RAF Commands.

Bob Nawarski began his work alongside the RAF as an Aircraftsman Second Class and was paid sixpence a day, then two shillings a day. He was sent to Blackpool for training:

> *They were all very friendly and started teaching us English straight away. Learning English was b***dy awful actually! I could not pronounce anything, no phonetic structure. Mill and mile always stumped me to begin with.*[5]

Józef Jaworzyn, experienced problems with his medical examination, which stated that he had a weak heart. He colluded with a friend to take a medical in his place and was eventually sent to Blackpool to train as a navigator:

> *It was easy to learn English technical language, but difficult to talk to people.*[6]

RAF technical guides and manuals were translated into Polish to help the newcomers adjust to their new surroundings. Józef recalled his training:

British RAF instructors were the best in the world, they really were fantastic. They were committed and extremely good with their pupils, and with us certainly.[7]

Instructors demonstrated patience and a high degree of discretion according to Józef, who had acquired a wild Polish friend during his training:

We had done acrobatics at a certain stage in the course, which was strictly forbidden. Upside down formation. He (the instructor) saw us and flew close enough to us to identify the aircraft and we were disciplined for this. He attributed our actions to being Polish and not understanding the transgression. We got voted average. I thought how dare they give me average when I know I was good! I was not at all grateful. I was not appreciative of the fact that we had been saved. If we had been English, we would have been thrown out of training.

Ten Rules for Air Fighting

1 Wait until you see the whites of his eyes. Fire short bursts of one to two seconds and only when your sights are definitely 'ON.'

2 Whilst shooting think of nothing else, brace the whole of the body; have both hands on the stick, concentrate on your ring sight.

3 Always keep a sharp look out. "Keep your finger out!"

4 Height gives YOU the initiative.

5 Always turn and face the attack.

6 Make your decisions promptly. It is better to act quickly even though your tactics are not the best.

7 Never fly straight and level for more than thirty seconds in the combat area.

8 When diving to attack always leave a proportion of your formation above to act as top guard.

9 INITIATIVE, AGGRESSION, AIR DISCIPLINE and TEAM-WORK are words that mean something in Air Fighting.

10 Go in quickly—Punch hard—Get out!

A.G. MALAN W/Cdr.
10/1/42 – 61 OTU (Operational Training Unit)

Source: RAF Museum Collection

I went to Oxfordshire with my close friend and started doing very well. I was one of the first to fly solo and became separated from my friend because he stayed wild and I was worried about the consequences of this. Some pilots were doing acrobatics, and some were flying under the Clifton suspension bridge. I lost two friends that way. They went and hit a tree and were killed.' Flying techniques related to the length of time one was a pilot. Being a pilot is only stage one, being a military pilot is stage two and being a confident military pilot is stage three. You needed to be confident in all weather conditions. I got my wings in Oxford and it later transpired that there was nothing wrong with my heart.[8]

Young aspiring airmen required training in all aspects of flying, but most of the Polish pilots were experienced and eager for combat. Frustrated by constant marching up and down airfields and impatient to get in the air, they spent their time pestering senior officers, as Bolesław Drobiński recalled:

We went to Blackpool and kept asking "When will we get to fly? The answer came back, don't worry, there is plenty of time.[9]

Adjutant to 307 Squadron Flight Lt. C.A. Hale wrote:

I remember arriving at Kirton in early September 1940, charged with the task of Adjutant to a Polish Squadron about to be formed. I have a vivid memory of the evening of 10th September 1940 at the railway station awaiting the arrival of the train from Blackpool with the Squadron personnel—Poles descending in large numbers from the train, and the search for an officer who could speak French! Thence to the aerodrome by lorry and getting everyone settled down for the night. English as a language was virtually non-existent at that point and French was the medium of communication. Then came the work of settling down as an Air Force Squadron.[10]

Canadian pilot Johnny Kent assigned to 303 Squadron, explained how, during training, language problems had the potential to interfere with combat operations:

I think perhaps the training period was unnecessarily prolonged and this certainly irked the Poles, who kept remonstrating with us that the best training was over France, but we still had to be quite sure they knew exactly how we operated. This was not always easy to get across as illustrated on one occasion when 'A' Flight was scheduled to act as

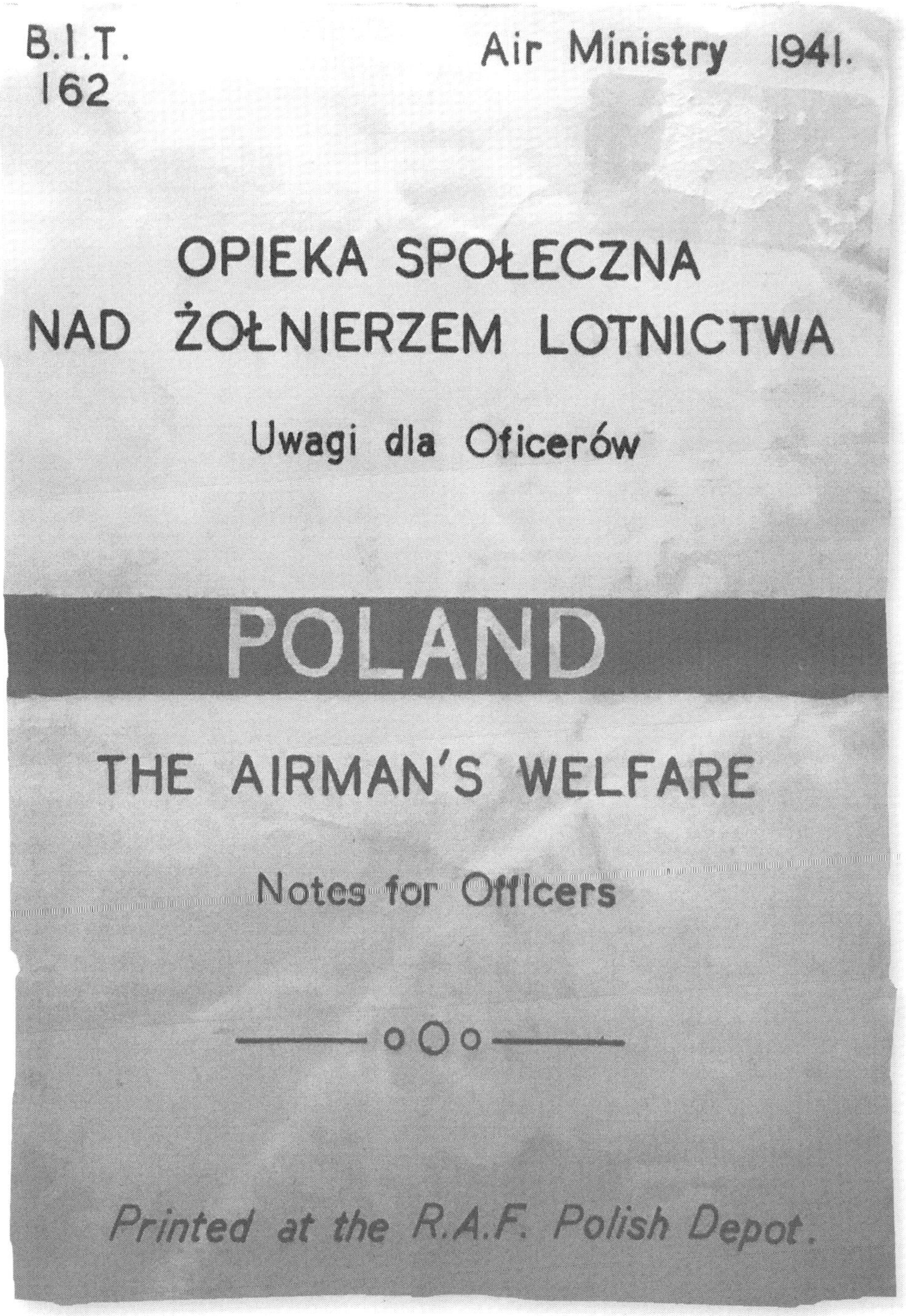

B.I.T.
162

Air Ministry 1941.

OPIEKA SPOŁECZNA
NAD ŻOŁNIERZEM LOTNICTWA

Uwagi dla Oficerów

POLAND

THE AIRMAN'S WELFARE

Notes for Officers

———— o O o ————

Printed at the R.A.F. Polish Depot.

*Above: Bilingual health and welfare guidance
for RAF and PAF officers.*

a formation of 'bombers' while 'B' Flight was to carry out an intercep-
tion and make dummy attacks on us. I explained this very carefully
and impressed upon them that no evasive action was to be taken as
we were simulating bombers depending upon crossfire for defence.
They all said that they fully understood and off we went. I led the flight
off to the west and climbed to height, then set off for Northolt. Just east
of Reading I saw the other flight diving down to attack and then, as
they completed the attack and started their break away, I was horrified
to see my number three, Flying Officer Ferić, pull up into a violent bar-
rel-roll and get right on the tail of one of the attacking Hurricanes. For-
tunately he recognized it just in time, as he was on the point of shooting
it down—he had completely misunderstood what I had said during
briefing, even though I had used an interpreter, and thought that we
were to be the attacking force. [11]

Dowding had initially planned to incorporate pairs of Polish pilots into existing Fighter squadrons but this policy failed to provide cohesive teams. Enthusiastic Polish airmen often broke formation in their eagerness to shoot down the enemy, undermining strategic tactical flying. Consequently, Dowding was forced to reconsider and establish homogenous units.

To emphasise the importance of flying in formation Polish pilots were required to cycle around airfields on specially adapted tricycles fitted with radio equipment. The Dowding system depended on aircraft being vectored onto the enemy by sector control rooms giving instructions by radio. An RAF tricycle unit was established, each tricycle was equipped with a radio and compass; and was used to train sector controllers in how to vector aircraft successfully and make interceptions. Trainee controllers operated from an off-site control room while airmen did the cycling on a parade ground. This system was simultaneously used to train Polish pilots in understanding English controllers' instructions. [12]

Undoubtedly experienced pilots found this process extremely tiresome and demeaning but newer, younger recruits recognised the value of such training. Bob Nawarski, who described himself as being a 'very green' nineteen-year old, when he first arrived as an auxiliary pilot at RAF Northolt in 1940 explained:

Close or loose formation flying was important. We were taught to fly in
a certain position and maintain it. If you take eight seconds off from
looking at the leader you can lose him. It's quite easy to get lost in the
air. You had to follow the leader exactly. If he suddenly turns off, you

don't know where he is. Operationally close formation was about twenty yards; in loose formation you were fifty yards away with more room for manoeuvre. [13]

RAF instructors frequently reported that the Poles' natural exuberance needed to be curtailed in order to maintain Squadron discipline and a sense of order.

Tadeusz Krzystek, who was a member of the PAF ground crew, quickly observed that both in theory and practice the RAF did things differently to Polish personnel.

Our pilots were brought up to fight straight away. They did not appreciate how the RAF worked, because strategy was only known at the top. I admired the English RAF and their attitudes to fighting the war, because it was a more visible struggle, which wasn't taken lightly. With ground crew, when it was necessary to change an engine our mechanics would take a new engine by the hand from a crate. The English would say wait for a crane because there is a risk of breaking your leg...not better or worse, but a different approach. Poles wanted to press on and not wait for a crane, but we learned! When our mechanics had finished the job NAFFI came up with a cup of tea. We became more anglicized. [14]

In addition to English language lessons, and instruction in flying and navigation techniques, Polish pilots were introduced to new, modern aircraft and tactical fighting strategies. Bob Nawarski recalled:

In France measurements were in metric and aircraft was old. The Hurricane was very responsive, different, stronger altogether...more guts. No comparison with planes you had flown before. Very manoeuvrable and very forgiving. If you made a mistake that could end up writing the aircraft off, you could remedy it quite quickly. As long as you were not too low you could get away with it, whereas with some aircraft you wouldn't. It was a lovely aircraft to fly. Variable pitch control, engage propeller, the finer the pitch the more bite you got into it. Flew more on giro because it was easier to use and more visible. Compass needle could swing ten degrees one way or another, setting the giro was more accurate and easier to maintain direction. You were taught to use guns while chasing aircraft. By the time bullets get to the enemy he will have moved, you had to aim ahead of the aircraft or anticipate his move. You needed to figure out distances. Ammunition was coloured white, blue or red (in training) so it would show whether

Above: *ASV Mk II front transmitter antenna on Consolidated Canso.*

> *you hit it (drogue) or not. We were taught tactical flying…for example,*
> *what your duties were if you were leader. The more violent your flying*
> *was the more difficult for formation.* [15]

For some Polish airmen, the introduction to modern aircraft was rudimentary. Bolesław Drobiński described his first encounter with a Spitfire:

> *We hadn't even seen a Spitfire before, so we went to a senior officer and*
> *he took us to show us quickly what's what. Each of us practised taking*
> *off and landing, that was our introduction to Spitfires! We were told to*
> *get acquainted with the terrain and find a reconnaissance point.*
> *Flying Spitfires was marvellous. The apex of flying, it reacted to the*
> *slightest movement. Hurricane was quicker in a dive and had a bigger*
> *cabin. Spitfire had a smaller cabin, but when you were belted in you*
> *felt like you were one with the aircraft. It was like a racing horse*
> *absolutely superb. The aristocrat of all fighter planes.* [16]

Changes in aircraft engines, design and weaponry continued throughout the war. Moreover, improvements in radar significantly enhanced the ability to detect the enemy. Training was ongoing therefore, and courses were continually adapted to take account of technological advances. However, weather conditions, flight times (day or night), the role of different Squadrons and the formation of German raids also influenced tactical approaches to aerial combat. As Wing Commander Ronald Kellett, who formed the Polish 303 Squadron pointed out:

The Germans had possibly recruited all their pilots from railway and tram drivers as they were at this point flying in very rigid formations, and Teutonic like they all had Fuhrers to follow! The first Squadron attack on a German formation showed me that the leaders of the close escort fighters were standing back and above the bombers so that they could see when our fighters were in contact with their bombers, but there was an area of 100 yards in front and 500 behind, below and on the flanks where they could see nothing. The obvious tactic was to dive in front of the fighters and make a feint on the bombers, pull up under the fighters and give the leaders of the close escort fighters a good burst of gun fire from underneath. This attack was immediately adopted by 'A' flight doing the feint while 'B' flight attacked the bombers. The result justified the tactic as almost immediately the close escort dived out of the battle leaving time not only for 'B' flight to attack the bombers, but for 'A' to follow 'B' flight on the tail of the enemy formation..

Although our attacks were successful and also proved sound from the point of view of our own casualties, we found that the enemy aircraft were slow to catch fire in spite of close-range firing. We had strict rules about scoring…the enemy aircraft had either to catch fire or hit the ground. There was little problem about knowing whether you were hitting the target as you could see the explosive bullets exploding on the enemy aircraft. About 1 in 5 of the bullets were de Wilde explosive, but because of self-sealing tanks and armour plating defending the German pilots, our sighting pattern seemed inadequate, so in spite of orders we aligned all our 8 guns to a point 200 yards dead ahead: this seemed more effective. [17]

From 1940 onwards fifteen Polish Squadrons were established and Polish pilots could be found in Fighter Command, Bomber Command and Coastal Command. Józef Jaworzyn, assigned to the latter following navigation training, noted that water deflection was a constant problem. Identifying and attacking German U-boats at night was also difficult. At times he was required to fly at 500ft during night hours without a search light, descending to 25ft when launching his attack. His main area of activity was over the Bay of Biscay. Eventually, 172 Squadron received Wellington aircraft which were installed with radar and search lights.

German U-boats usually surfaced at night to recharge their batteries: *Imagine their total surprise when, without warning, from out of the blackness they were bathed in a blinding light before being raked with machine-gun fire and straddled with depth charges. When coastal Command received its new centimetric air-to-surface-vessel radar (ASV MkIII) in 1943, it opened up a whole new way of intercepting surfaced U-boats in the darkness. Yet although ASV could locate the enemy vessel, when the aircraft closed in for the attack the 'blip' disappeared off the cathode ray tube due to interference from ground clutter. It was clear that some means of lighting up the night to enable identification of the*

Above: *Position of Leigh Light on Bristol Beaufighter.*

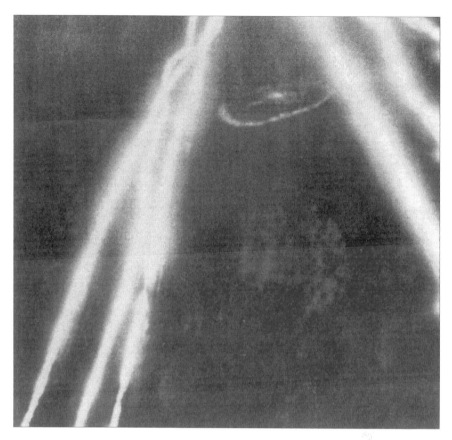

Above: *Destroyed U-boat illuminated by Leigh Light.*

*target and allow an attack to press home was needed urgently. Wing
Commander Humphrey de Verd Leigh, a son of the manse and a staff
officer at Coastal Command, devised his own solution to the problem,
which involved mounting a powerful, forward-pointing searchlight
underneath the aircraft.*[18]

This welcome innovation needed precise implementation as Jaworzyn recalled;

*Leigh developed a technique of combining radar and a visible way of
seeing U-boats. This required extensive training to coordinate the crew.
We were already orientated in the identification of ships. Once the U-
boat was detected we had to descend to the right height for the
searchlight to be operated...but not too high for the depth charges to be
dropped. Radio operator had to lead pilot the right way and so on,
while one of the crew operated the searchlight. Chances of hitting the*

water were great. Reflection could be deceptive. Early on there were lots of engine problems. You had 15 seconds to sort things out or you were pretty much finished. I do not know of any occasion when a Wellington XVI landed, and crew survived in the open sea. It was not an aircraft that could survive on water, it would break up. If you had cloud you put throttle on full and hope you could escape. Wellington XVI was a powerful aircraft but sometimes difficult to fly. Those who did best were the older crews who had trained most likely before the war. Crew that had experience and confidence were those who could perform and attack successfully.[19]

While engineering improvements and innovations were practical, tactical approaches to aerial combat were sometimes theoretical in nature, and occasionally controversial. Air-Vice Marshal Leigh Trafford-Mallory for instance, strongly advocated what became known as the 'Big Wing' theory. This necessitated the amalgamation of five squadrons flying in formation to intercept approaching German raids. Whereas Dowding believed that the use of smaller units of fighter aircraft, rapidly deployed, achieved better combat results. Since the 'Big Wing' theory delayed reaction times and only worked successfully on one occasion, Dowding's tactical approach proved in the long-term, to be superior and more effective.

Members of the Polish Air Force had different combat strategies; and in their eagerness to fight some would launch outstanding, daring, and usually triumphant 'lone wolf' attacks on enemy planes. They were also highly critical of the British tradition of flying in strict, close 'V' formation; a practice which left little room for manoeuvre. As Flight Commander Witold Urbanowicz observed:

While facing the enemy they flew like a parade in tight threes, one after another. Such a formation was wrong. Above all for the pilots this was making it difficult to observe air space as everyone had to watch his neighbour's plane to avoid collision. Apart from that, a squadron flying in such a tight formation was an easy and compact target for the enemy.[20]

German aircraft however were similarly confined in terms of manoeuvrability, because they also flew in rigid formation. As the war progressed valuable lessons were learned, and Wing Commanders adopted more flexible tactics. They further discovered that Polish pilots whether newly trained or combat hardened, generally possessed zeal, courage, skill and determination.

Homesick and concerned for the wellbeing of their families, they adjusted quickly to their new circumstances. They hated the over cooked vegetables served up by their Blackpool land ladies along with tasteless desserts of thick bland custard or stewed fruit. Neither were they fond of horizontal rain, and sea breezes which could rapidly turn into bitterly biting winds. However, they loved dancing at Blackpool's Winter Gardens, where they fervently wooed young girls with their good looks, attentiveness and charm. Many encounters at dance evenings were followed by lengthy kissing sessions and brief romances. Local girls were intrigued and excited by Polish men, who displayed courteous manners and spoke lovingly to them in stilted but endearing broken English. In fact, the mere presence of these handsome young Poles brightened the dreary monotony of black-outs and rationing. More importantly, they had arrived on British soil in time to significantly influence the outcome of the first battle in history to be decided by air power alone.

Chapter 3
The Battle of Britain Phases One, Two and Three

While Polish pilots were cycling around aerodromes and getting to grips with the English language, the Battle of Britain was already raging overhead. This crucial, aerial conflict began on 10th July 1940 when German raids targeted ports, ships and areas of aircraft production. During the following weeks these fierce enemy attacks increasingly focussed on RAF stations, runways, southern and eastern ports and industrial centres. Moreover, as Goering's Luftwaffe attempted to destroy British defences and decimate RAF Fighter Command in preparation for a German invasion, daylight raids intensified. Significantly, because France had collapsed so spectacularly in the face of German aggression Goering fully expected Britain to do likewise. German naval commanders however did not share his confidence.

Nevertheless, despite the conflicting views of his Chiefs of staff, on 21st July Hitler outlined the details of his proposed invasion of England, explaining the potential difficulties:

'This is not a case of a single crossing operation as in Norway; operational surprise cannot be expected; a defensively prepared and utterly determined enemy faces us and dominates the sea area which we must use. For the Army 40 divisions will be required; the most difficult part will be the continued reinforcement of material and stores. We cannot count on supplies of any kind being available to us in England. The prerequisites are complete mastery of the air, the operational use of powerful artillery in the Dover Straits and protection by mine fields. The time of the year is an important factor, since the weather in the North Sea and in the Channel during the second half of September is very bad and the fogs begin in the middle of October. The main operation will therefore have to be completed by the 15th of September.'[1]

Left: *Member of the Observer Corps on the rooftops of London, scanning the skyline for incoming enemy raids.*

At this stage Hitler firmly believed that a successful German invasion of Britain was a foregone conclusion. He was also convinced that Germany could easily win the war; dismissing those who failed to share his vision as pathetic imbeciles. Full of blustering rhetoric and misplaced confidence the Fuhrer claimed British people were merely too stubborn to accept the reality of German military supremacy. Yet he still attempted to elicit a British surrender and peppered major cities with propaganda material:

On 2nd August 1940 leaflets in place of bombs were dropped by a single enemy plane flying at considerable height. They fell in the Backwell district (Bristol) shortly after midnight. Headed 'A last Appeal to Reason –by A. Hitler, it was an English translation of Hitler's speech before the Reichstag 19th June 1940.[2]

Such an appeal was, of course, futile. A month later, on 2nd September, the highest scoring pilot of the Battle of Britain, Czechoslovakian born Josef František shot down a Bf 109E 5 kilometres East of Dover.[3] The first Polish pilots meanwhile had begun serving alongside the RAF on 16th July, and almost immediately made their mark with flying Officer Antoni Ostowicz, attached to the 145 Squadron, scoring the first Polish kill after only three days. Subsequently, for almost four weeks German fighter and bomber aircraft pummelled the ports and shipping routes around the coast of Britain. Portland naval base sustained serious damage on the 11th of August and some radar stations were rendered inoperable.

In a determined bid to wipe out Fighter Command, Luftwaffe raids escalated in number from 13th August onward. Known as Eagle Day in Germany this day was supposed to mark a turning point in Luftwaffe fortunes. In total, 485 German bomber and 1,000 fighter aircraft embarked on their offensive missions during the afternoon alone. RAF Fighter Command responded by mounting 727 sorties. Subsequently, Germany launched unremitting aerial attacks by day and night on southern England, inflicting serious damage on RAF aerodromes and sector stations. Ferocious 'dog fights' ensued above the English Channel as pilots from 11 group dispersed wave after wave of enemy bomber formations, downing as many as possible and sustaining considerable losses. There were many phenomenal acts of bravery. Flight Lieutenant James Nicholson for instance, continued to shoot down enemy aircraft even when the cockpit of his Hurricane was engulfed by flames following an attack from a Messerschmitt Bf110. He was awarded the Victoria Cross for his outstanding courage.[4] By far the hardest day of fighting however, occurred on the 18th of

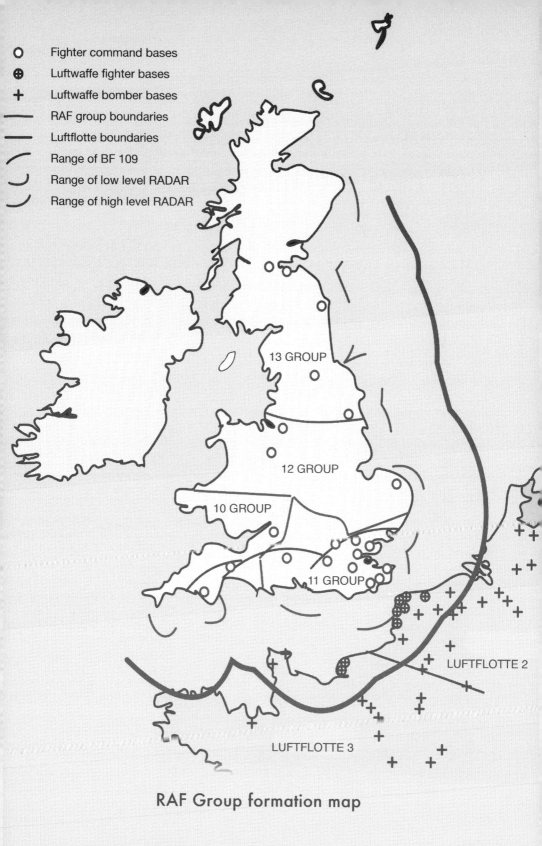

RAF Group formation map

August. On this day at 1300 hrs the Luftwaffe mounted a huge offensive on Biggin Hill and Kenley airfields. This was followed by attacks on North Weald, a radar station at Poling, a coastal command base at Thorney island and Hornchurch. In total, the Luftwaffe launched eight hundred and fifty missions involving two thousand two hundred air crew, they lost 69 aircraft. The RAF and Fleet Air Arm had responded with nine hundred and twenty-seven missions involving six hundred air crew, their losses totalled 68 aircraft. With such sustained, harrowing and damaging enemy raids RAF sector stations were beginning to suffer, to the point where the efficiency of Fighter Command was undermined. Pilots were exhausted and it was becoming increasingly difficult for the RAF to replace those who had been killed or severely injured. Government ministers debated the prospect of reducing pilot training periods and aircraft production was stepped up.

Given this dire situation the timely injection of Polish pilots into RAF Command forces was significant. The Polish 302 Squadron entered the fray on the 15th

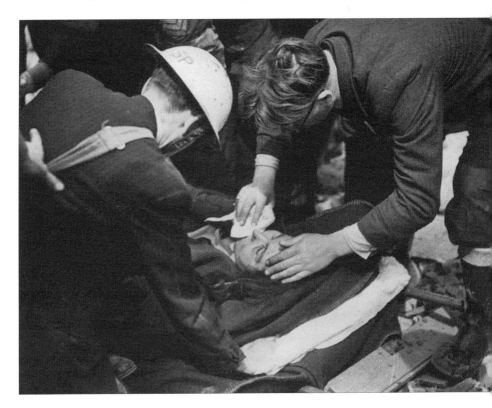

Above: ARP warden and first aiders attend to Blitz victim.

Top left: Hawker Hurricanes in formation above Kent.
Lower left: Spitfires and He111 during Battle of Britain 1940.

August attached to number twelve group. They were charged with the responsibility of supporting eleven group and relieving their hard-pressed squadrons when necessary. Elsewhere, Polish pilots were assigned to other RAF units to replace injured personnel. They instantly fought with distinction. Sergeant Antoni Głowacki for example, assigned to 501 Squadron, downed five German bombers during his three combat missions on 24th August; achieving the rare distinction of becoming an 'Ace in a Day.'[5]

Then, on 30th of August another Polish airman, Ludwik Paszkiewicz, acting on his own initiative, shot down a German aircraft during a training flight. Flying with the newly formed 303 Squadron on a routine interception exercise he sighted the enemy and reported it to his Commanding Officer Squadron Leader Kellett. Since there was no response from Kellett he chased the enemy and opened fire from approximately two hundred yards distance. The aircraft (an Me 110) plunged to the ground and caught fire. On his return to RAF Northolt Paszkiewicz was simultaneously disciplined for breaking formation and praised for achieving the Squadron's first kill. The following morning 303 Squadron became operational and was assigned to number eleven group. Almost a year since the German invasion of their native land the Poles were finally equipped with powerful aircraft and enough ammunition to fight the enemy. As Flight Commander Johnny Kent of 'A' Flight recalled:

There was not long to wait until the first scramble order came through and away went the Squadron led by Ronald Kellett. After some vectoring about, they intercepted a formation of Messerschmitt 109's. Kellett immediately attacked and in a matter of minutes six German

Above: Artwork drawn by members of 307 Squadron.

fighters were destroyed. It was a wonderful opening to what was to be a fantastic six weeks.[6]

Kent was on leave when this action took place but was scrambled with his men a few days later:

I was leading the Squadron and we were soon over Manston at 19,000 feet—having the greatest difficulty in hearing the controller as we were at extreme range. I did hear a warning of 'bandits' (any enemy aircraft, as opposed to a 'bogey' which was an unidentified subject) in our vicinity, but as I almost immediately intercepted a Squadron of Hurricanes, I put it down to mistaken identity. Within a minute or two I turned south and, looking up, saw nine 109's diving on us out of the sun. I turned into the attack and Sergeant Rogowski, who was doing search formation behind, pulled up and went head on into the middle of them, closely followed by František. The German formation split up and a general melee ensued, grey shapes with black crosses on them flashed past only feet away, next the brown and green of a Hurricane flashed across the sights. Streams of grey tracer smoke criss-crossed the sky in all directions. It was impossible to hold a steady aim and snap shooting was the order of the day, but so confused was the fight that one had little or no chance to see if one's fire had taken effect before having to take wild evasive action to avoid either the enemy's fire or a collision.[7]

When this fight was over Kent re-joined three of his own pilots and flew home, not knowing the whereabouts of the remainder of his Squadron. Watching eagerly for their return he stated:

The missing ones came drifting in at intervals after we had landed, three of them doing victory rolls as they pulled up over the dispersal. Rogowski and František had got one each which I had witnessed just before the two formations really tangled. Henneberg had chased a109 ten miles into France before he managed to shoot it down; he then had to turn for home but found his victim's number two was on to him. After a brief encounter Henneberg succeeded in destroying this 109 also.

It was all very satisfactory as, despite the tactical advantage the enemy had enjoyed, they had lost four destroyed and one probably destroyed, this one by Ferić who then suffered engine failure and had had to land near Manston. As he glided down, Rogowski saw that he was in trouble and went down with him to protect him from attack. This readiness to help a stricken comrade was a feature amongst the Poles that I was to witness on several occasions, and it was good to know they possessed it.[8]

Polish pilots in other Squadrons meanwhile, continued to fight with great skill. Super vigilant combat veteran, Stanisław Skalski of the 501 Squadron for instance, shot down a Heinkel on 30th August, an Me 109 the following day and two more on 2nd of September.

Moreover, from the outset, it was clear that Polish airmen were determinedly and fiercely aggressive, zooming in on enemy aircraft decisively and fearlessly. Flying east of Biggin Hill at 18.25 hrs. on 31st August with the enemy flying at 14000 feet, Pilot Officer Ferić of 303 Squadron shot down an Me 109. His combat report recorded:

*After about 15 minutes we saw about 70 E/A (enemy aircraft) to N.E.
On the way towards them Yellow section met 3 Me 109s, which did not
see us as we had the sun behind us. The surprise was complete. Each of
us took one E/A. A higher section of Me 109s began to descend on us. I
gave a short burst at my Me 109 from 70 yards at fuselage and engine.
The pilot baled and E/A crashed in flames.*
(Note: P/O Ferić fired only 20 rounds from each gun)[9]

A further report written on 6th September, when Ferić was flying above
Sevenoaks in Kent at 0900 hrs stated:

*I was Yellow 3. Flying to the south of Farnborough I noticed 20-30 enemy
bombers to the right of my course at a height of about 20,000 ft. and
about 60 enemy fighters about 3000 ft. above the bombers. Yellow
Leader changed his course and prepared to attack. In the meantime,*

***Above:** Polish Airmen attending Holy Mass.*

Above: Spitfire Mk II

*E/A dived and attacked us. I found myself engaged in a dog fight in
which were also taking part Spitfires. Suddenly a ME 109 painted white
from his nose to the end of the cockpit zoomed up. I caught him head
on and fired 3 short bursts at 200-250 yds. He burst into flames and fell
to the ground.* [10]

This encounter occurred on one of the worst combat days for 303 Squadron.
Scrambled at 0840hrs nine Hurricanes left Northolt and flew over western Kent.
In doing so they confronted massive formations of enemy aircraft flying to
the east of them and above. To compound matters, operations control officials
had misinformed air crew of the enemy bombers' altitude. This situation
immediately placed 303 Squadron at a disadvantage, as Intelligence Officer
E. M. Hadwin explained in an official secret report compiled for Fighter
Command:

Their lack of height forced them to attack climbing, and at only 140 m.p.h.
and contributed very largely to our heavy casualties.

S/L. Kellett's report states:

*"This was the biggest formation I have ever seen. It covered an area 20
miles x 5. There were many big planes, Dorniers, He, 111, and some
four engined. There were the usual Me 110's among them, and
formations of Me 109's up to 25,000ft. fully 300 to 400 E/A. I
manoeuvred to do a quarter head on attack on the bombers. I put a
long burst into the port engine of a DO.215, and saw it commence to*

Above: Hurricane roaring across Bristol Fighter Station.

smoke. Then I did a quarter astern attack and the engine caught fire. Just as I was about to break away a series of explosions took place in my aircraft. After diving, I realized that it was very difficult to control the aircraft as there was a very big hole in the starboard wing, and the aircraft was flying with starboard wing very low. There was no elevator control and not much rudder control. I managed to get the aircraft down to 140 m.p.h. and keep it under control with the stick hard back and over to port. Finding Biggin Hill close, I made a landing with the under carriage down, but without flaps."[11]

Enemy casualties consisted of 1 DO.215, 5 Me. 109s, and 1 He.111 destroyed and two Me. 109's probable. This tally came at a heavy price with 303 Squadron sustaining category three damage (aircraft written off) to five Hurricanes, and category two damage (aircraft in need of serious repair) to one Hurricane. Two pilots were seriously injured and two slightly wounded. Hadwin continued his summary for Fighter Command:

The report of F/O Urbanowicz is typical of the rest of the Squadron:

"I was with Yellow 2 with S/L Krasnodębski, the second section. I saw a raid a mile away travelling westward about 40 Dorniers. Red section went into attack. I saw Me 109's and Hurricanes flying across from left to right on each other's tails. One Me. then attacked me from starboard.

Above: Stanisław Skalski (front left) pictured with the wing of an enemy aircraft, and fighter pilots at Filton near Bristol

We had a short dog fight. I fired for 3 or 4 seconds at 200 yards. The engine caught fire and E/A fell vertically to earth. I lost my section and orbited. I saw bombs dropping in one place and Me. 109's circling around that place and much A.A. fire. I circled there too and attacked a bomber. One Me. 109 was in the way and two more attacked me. I had to dog fight with the 3 Me's. I had no chance to fire. I escaped over some balloons by the sea, and the Me's climbed up. I heard 'Apany Pancake and I came home.[12]

In addition to the problems associated with altitude, many of the pilots needed to fly towards the sun to engage the enemy, which temporarily obscured their visibility. Communications were also virtually non-existent because of radio/telephone interference. Concluding his report Hadwin stated::

As soon as the Squadron went into attack large numbers of Me. 109's dived down from many directions, and the Squadron broke up. Interference on the R/T had been bad and intercommunication in the Squadron was impossible. Stories of the rest of the Squadron are as follows:

F/Lt. Forbes shot down one Me 109 and damaged another. He was forced down by petrol pouring into the cockpit. He tried to land but overshot the field. He was slightly wounded by splinters. The aircraft was damaged by shell fire and by the crash and is Cat 3. F/O Ferié destroyed one Me. 109 and probably another. Sgt František shot down one Me. 109 and his aircraft was hit in the tail by shell. He landed at Northolt and his aircraft has been repaired here. S/L

Above: ***Hawker Hurricane***

Krasnodębski's aircraft was hit by shell before he had engaged the enemy, and immediately caught fire. He baled and the aircraft crashed in flames. He is in Farnborough hospital suffering from burns and shock. Sgt. Karubin claims to have shot down one He. 111. He crashed near Pembury shot down by a Me. 109 and is in Pembury hospital. His injuries are understood to be slight, and he will shortly return to duty.[13]

Communication problems stemming from errors made in operations rooms were infrequent, but when they did occur, they could place a Squadron in extreme danger, as Johnny Kent noted:

The situation became confused in the operations room by the large number of raids on the board and the controller ordered both 'A' Flight and 'B' Flight to 'stand by,' but separately. Within a minute or two he scrambled first one then the other without realizing what he had done. He kept giving me vectors to intercept and it dawned on me that, from his instructions he thought the two flights were together as a squadron. I did not want to compromise security by telling him this on the R/T in clear but—when he said: "Garta to Apany Red Leader, vector one-four-zero Angels one-five, one hundred and fifty plus twenty miles ahead—over!" I felt that the time had come. "Apany Red Leader to Garta," I replied, "Understand one-fifty plus twenty miles ahead—you realize we are only six, I repeat six—over." "Apany Red Leader from Garta," came the cheery reply. "Understand you are only six; very well, be careful!" I could have shot him![14]

Ceaseless large-scale enemy raids on RAF ground installations had inflicted serious damage on southern bases and ports. But despite being outnumbered, Fighter Command pilots fought valiantly night and day, destroying and damaging Luftwaffe aircraft in unexpected numbers. Between 26th August and 6th September, the RAF had lost 248 aircraft compared to Luftwaffe losses of 322 aircraft. Yet, an over-confident Goering believed his air force to be on the verge of victory. He gleefully told his commanders therefore, that the RAF had less than a hundred fighter aircraft and were unable to protect London because all southern airfields had been destroyed. Influenced by this delusion he decided that the time was right for the Luftwaffe to focus bombing raids on the British capital.

Chapter 4

The Battle of Britain
Phases Four and Five

Londoners were enjoying a warm, sunny afternoon on 7th September 1940. They were picnicking in parks, leisurely walking along busy streets, attending matinee performances at cinemas and generally going about their business as usual. Then, at 16.43 hours the air raid warning siren signalled incoming German bombers. Guided to London's industrial heartland by the river Thames they dropped their incendiary bombs across factories, warehouses and the docks. These started fires which further guided the bombers to their targets. The whole of London's East End was ablaze within an hour. With terrifying crashes and thunderous noise high explosive bombs landed on both sides of the river Thames. Buildings split and shattered under the violent onslaught and the ground convulsed. The Ford motor factory at Dagenham, West and East India Docks, and Woolwich were on fire. Streets were overrun with rats trying to flee bombed out warehouses and factories, and East End rail links were destroyed. In addition, power supplies were disrupted. Dead and injured people were blasted onto the roofs of buildings and vehicles. At 18.30 hours, the bombers turned to head back to their airfields in France, then a mere two hours later a further harrowing onslaught began, an intense air raid that continued throughout the night.[1] Over 400 people were killed on this first night of the blitz with hundreds more severely injured. Subsequently, except for one night, London was raided by day or night for fifty-six consecutive dates.[2]

Combat records for 7th September estimated that there were at least forty Dornier 215 aircraft and fifty Me 109's flying at 20,000 feet during the initial attack on London. When they were first detected on radar RAF personnel were prepared once again to protect their airfields. In a matter of minutes however, they realized the capital was the target and launched a brisk response. Despite overwhelming numbers of German fighters and bombers RAF and PAF pilots bravely intercepted the raids:

One formation took a fierce drubbing from Duxford and Northolt pilots (including the 303 Polish Squadron) on its way out. As the enemy had steadily converged in one direction for an hour and a half no less than twenty-one of the twenty-three squadrons, we sent up succeeded in engaging. German losses were therefore severe –forty aircraft against twenty-eight of ours. Their powerful escorts however, had safeguarded German bombers and nearly all the machines shot down by our pilots were fighters.[3]

On this horrendous day 303 Squadron shot down fourteen German planes and made four possible hits in one mission in defence of London, without sustaining any losses. In the aftermath of combat, Intelligence Officer Hadwin called several hospitals for news of the injured. After speaking to one matron he recorded the fate of a young Polish airman who had engaged the enemy at 1700 hours while flying over Essex:

I learn that Pilot Officer J. Daszewski has dictated a report stating that he brought down one DO215 destroyed, and probably another (one engine in flames) his aircraft was hit by shells. When it caught fire, he baled-out, seriously wounded near Canterbury Gate, and his A/C (aircraft) fell in flames nearby.[4]

Above: *Members of 303 Squadron at RAF Northolt.*

In the heat of battle, it was often difficult to estimate numbers of enemy aircraft and in the first raid alone, at least two hundred bombers wreaked havoc across London. However, the process of shifting Luftwaffe attention away from bombing RAF installations onto the bombing of major cities and industrial centres proved to be a massive German strategic error; because it afforded the RAF some much needed respite in which to replace and repair damaged aircraft, rest pilots and strengthen resources. Moreover, Dowding introduced a stabilisation scheme on the 8th September, which regrouped squadrons according to pilot experience. Inclement weather also reduced the number of raids in the following few days. Training periods for pilots were shortened from one month to a fortnight to quickly replace those who had been killed or injured but Dowding feared their lack of combat experience could hamper operations. Despite these reservations, Fighter Command remained determinedly robust in their objectives, and according to Bolesław Drobiński the morale in 303 Squadron was excellent:

> *Nobody suffered with a lack of moral fibre. One pilot was shot down and baled-out. He parachuted into the channel and got into a dinghy about five or six miles from the English coast. He suddenly found himself in the morning going in the opposite direction. He was three nights in the dinghy and eventually picked up by a British trawler. He was quite happy.*[5]

While the shortage of experienced pilots remained a concern, at least British aircraft production was outstripping that of Germany; with four hundred and sixty fighter aircraft rolling off the production lines every month, compared to Germany's monthly output of one hundred and eighty aircraft. Therefore, although the German High Command believed intelligence sources which claimed that the RAF was on its last legs, nothing could be further from the truth.

Furthermore, Polish pilots assigned to 300 Squadron Bomber Command were making sure that German invasion barges were prevented from crossing the English Channel. As the following combat reports from 14th September 1940 reveal:

> *F/O Suliński, F/O Bujalski and Sgt. Biezunski took off at 18.55 hrs – mission—the bombing of barges and shipping in Boulogne harbour. On Target: 20.43 hrs—20.46hrs. Level 10,000 feet. Pilot dropped 4 x 250 lb. bombs. Bombing results not observed owing to intense searchlight activity. Air gunner machine gunned searchlight station, being*

***Above:** Polish Fighter Pilots.*

*immediately extinguished. Aircraft landed at Digby 23.49 hrs.
F/O Antonowicz, P/O Dej and Sgt Kowalski took off at 1900 hrs.
On Target: 20.46 hrs—20.49 hrs. Level 10,000 feet. Pilot dropped 4 x 250 lb
bombs and two flares, results not observed. Aircraft landed 22.45 hrs.
P/O Jasiński, Sgt. Sobieszczuk and Sgt. Łapot took off at 19.05 hrs. Level
8,000 feet. Pilot dropped 4 x 250lb bombs, results not observed. Aircraft
landed at Newton 23.15 hrs.*[6]

Since German intelligence reports continued to underestimate the strength of
RAF Squadrons Luftwaffe bomber and fighter pilots were extremely shocked,
and somewhat bewildered on the morning of 15th September, to be confronted
by large numbers of Hurricanes and Spitfires as they approached the English
coastline. One in five of the courageous pilots who took off from RAF bases to
defend Britain on this day were Polish.

Flying Officer Julian Roch Kowalski described his call to arms:

Attention, attention. All Hurricane Squadrons scramble. Atmosphere has boiled up. The noise of the ignited machine engines and we are taking off in order: Canadians, Poles, Czechs. I fly on the left side of 302 commander Squadron Leader Satchell, Tadzio Czerwiński on his right. We went through the clouds. I squinted upwards. In the blue sky, hundreds of white trails scatter in great disorder, and lines straight, semi-circular and full circles cover the beautiful blue sky; some suddenly break and in a vertical, spiral, blue trail of smoke connect the sky with the ground. Every now and then white balloons open up there; it all looks like a great Christmas decoration suspended under a dome of sky. The combat is already on—I thought, Spitfires are welcoming the Me-109s. Below us white, neat puffy clouds, and formations of black German bombers against that background. Some are already scattered by Squadrons of Hurricanes and several are heading back south in disorder, but still more and more appear on the horizon. Great noise in my headphones. I am not listening, why should I? I don't understand anything anyway. Suddenly a voice in Polish shouting 'Attack! Kill them bastards!' That was Northolt I thought. They were closer, we are flying almost on top of them. Terrible view. I am glad I am not a German. We carry on. Meanwhile a large formation of Dorniers approached us, and after a moment I can hear the voice of Bader: 'Tally Ho!' The whole wing almost simultaneously made a sharp turn and went down at full throttle onto the tight formation of Dorniers. I did not go down to attack. I just got on the tail of one and fired a long burst straight into its fuselage from a minimum distance, and the Dornier continued to fly as before. I gave it a thought and shouted loudly: 'Roch, aim at the engine!' After a short burst from my guns the engine exploded, almost the entire wing fell off and the German disappeared, spinning under the clouds. I was sure that its crew would miss their lunch today. I then aimed at another one. Suddenly a Spitfire falling vertically literally cut a Dornier in half with its wing. The attack of Bader's wing must have been very effective as after just one kill I could not find another.[7]

Pilot Officer 'Tolo' Łokuciewski also shared his account:

We approached but enemy aircraft turned, and we attacked them from a deflected angle from the rear and above, but at that moment we ourselves were attacked from the rear by Me 109s. At the same time, I noticed another formation of enemy aircraft flying towards London, protected by Me 109s and 110s. I broke away and attacked the Me 109s with another section of Hurricanes. After firing a few bursts, a Me 109 began to smoke and eventually burst into flames. I was then hit from the rear by a cannon shell and landed wounded.[8]

Łokuciewski aged twenty-three, managed to land at Northolt before losing consciousness in his cockpit. He was dragged out of his damaged aircraft by ground crew and quickly transferred to hospital. Surgeons were able to remove some metal fragments from his legs, but many remained in situ.

Above: Bolesław Drobinski.

Above: 303 Squadron with number of enemy aircraft destroyed on the fuselage.

Sergeant Andruszków meanwhile shared a Dornier kill with another Pole, reporting that: *While returning to Northolt flying as Red 2 with Sgt. Wojciechowski we saw a DO. 215 lower and to our right. We both attacked and watched him fall in flames to the ground.*[9]

The first enemy formation had been sighted by Chain Home at about 11am and consisted of approximately one hundred fighters and bombers. This was followed by the sighting of another huge formation of around one hundred and fifty enemy aircraft at 13.45 between Dover and Dungeness. Indeed, combat reports clearly state that the afternoon raid consisted of around four hundred enemy aircraft.

Pilot Officer Mirosław Ferić, flying with 303 Squadron A Flight, intercepted both raids. His first report records:

After an hour's flight looking for E/A I was attacked by two ME's 109's over Dungeness. These were reinforced by three other ME's and in the ensuing fight I shot one down, firing a long burst from a distance of 300 yards. Being myself engaged I could not follow subsequent flight of damaged E/A, but F/Lt. Kent who was in the vicinity states that he saw the E/A burst into flames and fall to earth.[10]

Above: Polish Priest conducting a church service for Polish Airmen in Exeter.

Ferié delivered this attack at 12.00 hrs between South London and Hastings and estimated that there were about eighty enemy aircraft flying at 18,000 feet—a mix of Dornier 215's ME 109's and ME 110's.

At 1500 hrs Ferié confronted another tidal wave of enemy bombers and fighters and delivered another attack:

At a height of 18,000 feet S.E of Gravesend we intercepted about 150 to 200 E/A. After attacking the bombers, I was engaged by ME 109's and 110's. Since I had used up half my ammunition in attacking enemy bombers, I approached to about 100 to 80 yards before firing a burst at a ME 110, which immediately burst into flames and fell into the clouds out of control. Having now used up all my ammunition I took cover in the clouds and after a few minutes landed at Gravesend where I refuelled and returned to Northolt.[11]

Ferić combat report states that although 303 Squadron A Flight intercepted between one hundred and fifty and two hundred enemy aircraft, the total number intercepted by RAF Squadrons amounted to four hundred enemy aircraft. Ferić landed safely at Northolt, his Hurricane had sustained category one damage.

It was clear that Goering had decided to throw everything he had at the RAF in a concerted bid to make way for the invasion. Moreover, while Squadrons of valiant pilots ferociously defended Britain in sensational dog fights in the skies above, those on the ground became increasingly aware that this conflict was more intense. Monica Baly, a nurse with Princess Mary's Royal Air Force Nursing Service (PMRAFNS) witnessed the dramatic battle overhead:

It was a golden September day, the sea was blue and calm, and I was home on leave from hospital in Bexhill, having obtained the permit which confirmed that Bexhill was my home in what was now a defence zone. Our house was almost on the sea front, which was protected by barbed wire and concrete blocks, and mother was an A.R.P. warden. Always on the look-out for a supplement to our diet, mother and I decided to take a picnic to Fairlight Glen above Hastings and look for blackberries. We climbed up the deserted path and sat down and surveyed the serenity of the English Channel, never had it looked so beautiful. Then, in the distance we heard the sound of aircraft—ours or theirs? Suddenly the sky was full of activity, we sat transfixed, waves of planes came over, sometimes we could see the markings and there unfolded before our eyes perhaps the greatest battle of the Second World War. There above us were Spitfires and Hurricanes intercepting with bursting gun fire, then one would see a plane on fire spiralling down to the sea. Was this it? Was this the dreaded invasion?

We reckoned we were as safe on the cliff as anywhere but thought we ought to get home as soon as possible as best we could, so, forgetting the blackberries, we clambered back down the path only to find Hastings in confusion. No-one was sure what was happening overhead. Now our one thought was to get home to the wireless where the voice of Charles Gardiner in a legendary commentary gave an eye-witness account of what had happened and what was happening. Curiously, though one was chilled by the tragedy of burning aircraft which we had seen with out very eyes there was a sense of intense excitement. Later Gardiner was criticised for being carried away with emotion and making the whole thing sound like a football match, but that is how it seemed at the time. What we had witnessed was the pride of the Luftwaffe being picked off by some 300 Spitfires and Hurricanes.[12]

This pivotal, breath-taking aerial conflict was a defining turning point in the Battle of Britain. RAF pilots had shot down sixty-one German planes, and lost thirty-one. German pilots returned to their French bases defeated and deflated. During the evening 300 Squadron bombarded what remained of German invasion barges:

> W/cdr Makowski, F/O Rogalski and Sgt Gędziorowski took off at 18.55 hrs.
> On Target: 20.40 hrs—20.43 hrs. Shallow dive from 9,500 to 8,000 feet. Pilot dropped 4 x 250lb bombs in stick. Results not observed. Aircraft landed at 22.35 hrs.
> F/O Gębicki, Sgt Morawa and Sgt Egierski took off at 19.05 hrs.
> On Target: 20.43 hrs—20.48 hrs. Dive bombing from 7,000 to 5,500 feet. Pilot dropped two salvoes of two bombs (250lb) from 3,000 feet, firing with front and rear guns at searchlights in the harbour. Results of bombing not observed. Aircraft landed at 22.45 hrs.
> F/O Kałuża, F/O Chrostowski and Sgt Urbanowicz took off at 1900 hrs.
> On Target: 20.46 hrs—20.49 hrs. Level 9,000 feet. Observer dropped bombs in stick 4 x 250lb. Results not observed. Aircraft landed 22.40 hrs.
> F/Lt Kryński, P/O Szymański and Sgt. Graczyk took off at 19.00 hrs.
> On Target: 20.49hrs—2052hrs. Level 8,000 feet. Pilot dropped bombs in stick—three bombs hung up. Aircraft landed 22.45 hrs.
> P/O Kula, Sgt. Przbylski and Sgt. Kudełko took off at 19.05 hrs.
> On Target: 20.55 hrs. Shallow dive from 11,00 feet to 9,000 feet. Pilot dropped 4 x250lb bombs. Results not observed. Aircraft landed at 23.00hrs.
> Sgt. Kuflik, P/O Koziński and Sgt Artymiuk took off at 19.10 hrs.
> On Target: 20.55 hrs—20.58 hrs. No bombs dropped—pilot error.[13]

Clearly the winning combination of RAF Fighter, Bomber and Coastal Commands had triumphed over the Luftwaffe. In the face of such a decisive British victory Hitler was forced to abandon Operation Sea Lion. By the end of September, the Luftwaffe had lost 1,408 aircraft, compared with the RAF's loss of 697 aircraft. Angered and seriously thwarted Hitler increased the number of bombing raids on major British cities, while simultaneously redoubling German efforts in the Battle of the Atlantic. In October he met up with his bombastic ally Mussolini at Brenner Pass to discuss war strategies. Daylight raids over London began to subside but night bombing continued unabated.

Throughout September and October enemy raids on aircraft production areas were also stepped up. On 25th September Germans launched a daylight raid on Bristol aeroplane company:

> *Enemy planes dropped one hundred and sixty-eight bombs in forty-five seconds. Blenheims, Beauforts and Beaufighters were being constructed at BAC at this time. A German news agency claimed that: 'This factory will not produce many more aircraft.' But only eight planes were so seriously damaged as to be irreparable, and there was minor damage to twenty-four aircraft. Water and gas mains were affected and great western rail lines between Filton and Patchway were blocked.*[14]

Two days later the Germans initiated another daylight offensive against Bristol and were intercepted by a fearless 501 Squadron:

> *Germans came over with the same intentions as before—this time about 11.30am. A force of about nine bombers accompanied by fighters came over the city, but a Squadron of Hurricanes was waiting for them. Anti-aircraft guns were in action as well, and the formation was dispersed before it could reach its target. One Messerschmitt was brought down and fell in a yard in Stapleton Institute Fishponds.*[15]

As a major distribution centre, railway junction, port and aircraft manufacturer Bristol became a prime target for German bombers during the blitz on major cities. However, there appeared to be some miscalculations in German reconnaissance information and on many occasions German pilots dropped bombs in the Cardiff area believing they were dropping them on Bristol. The British also developed the art of deceiving German bombers. For instance, the practice of illuminating the hill tops of Horse-Shoe Pass in North Wales, offered some protection to nearby Liverpool and Manchester, since German pilots mistakenly believed the hill tops to be urban areas.

Naval bases were also a prime target for the Luftwaffe. Sergeant Andruszków of 'A' Flight 303 Squadron intercepted a raid and delivered an attack over Portsmouth on 26th September 1940:

Following my leader, I attacked the last HE 111 in a formation ¾ from the rear. I then climbed and saw a DO 215 to my left which I attacked. E/A dived, and I followed and fired several bursts from a very short distance. E/A continued his dive and crashed into the sea. I was then attacked by ME 109 which zoomed over me and I followed, but as he continued to draw away, I was unable to fire and turned. 1289 rounds of ammunition fired.[16]

Andruszków shot down one HE 111 flying at 16,000 feet. The following day Pilot Officer Ferić delivered an attack at 09.20 hrs over Horsham, shooting down one ME 109 and one HE111, his Hurricane sustained category three damage. His combat report stated:

Fifteen minutes after taking off we met enemy bomber formation. My Squadron engaged the protecting fighters. I attacked an ME 109, And after a short burst E/A burst into flames and crashed to earth. I then approached the bombers who were already being attacked by some of our aircraft. I attacked a HE and fired three short bursts. The pilot was evidently killed as the machine dived without smoke or flames and crashed between Croydon and Gatwick. As my aircraft had been hit by machine gun bullets I returned to Northolt.[17]

On 5th October 303 Squadron intercepted a raid of one hundred and fifty ME 110'S and ME 109'S. Ferić shot down one ME 110 near Rochester. This time the enemy planes were flying between 20,000 and 30,000 feet:

Over Kent we engaged ME 109's. Meanwhile it was noted that ME 110's, were also in the vicinity flying in a defensive circle. As ME 110's were above us we began to climb. I then noticed an ME 110 break away from the circle, and diving, make towards the sea, smoking slightly, but maintaining a very high speed. I chased E/A and catching up with him about seven miles from the coast fired a burst from a distance of about twenty yards into his cockpit. E/A immediately dived into the sea. Returning I saw 6/7 ME 110 and above them a number of ME 109's. 146 rounds of ammunition fired.[18]

Enemy raids peaked in mid-October and most included at least one hundred and fifty bombers. Squadrons from eleven group were scrambled on average

Above: *Group Captain Johnny Kent, nicknamed Kentowski by his Polish comrades, pictured with members of the Polish 303 Squadron.*

three or four times a day and as weather conditions deteriorated flying became more dangerous. During a daylight encounter on 29th October Luftwaffe losses amounted to twenty aircraft and it became glaringly obvious, even to the delusional Goering that German efforts to wipe out the RAF were futile.

The defensive Battle of Britain had been won and the threat of imminent invasion rescinded. Polish pilots, far from home, with no idea of what was happening to their families and loved ones, were the exceptional, triumphant stars of the conflict. In six frantic weeks members of 303 Polish Squadron had shot down a total of one hundred and twenty-six aircraft, with the loss of only eight pilots. This made them the highest scoring Squadron in Fighter Command. Since their phenomenal flying prowess was unrivalled, RAF pilots were quick to lavish praise on their Polish comrades, including Squadron Leader Douglas Bader who stated:

Left: Satirical drawing of Hitler consulting a fortune teller during the Battle of Britain.

So far as we were concerned, we loved our Polish allies. They were gallant and dedicated to destroying the enemy in the air. On the ground they were gay and amusing, sometimes tragic and forever loyal. It was a privilege to know them. They added lustre to the cause of freedom for which we were all fighting.[19]

In the aftermath of the Battle of Britain there was much debate as to why Polish pilots had achieved such spectacular success. Certainly, Poles were more reliant on their perceptive vision in combat than on radio communication. For instance, they were renowned for being able to spot enemy formations while they were still mere dots on the horizon. Evidently, in addition to their super vigilant visual awareness and flying expertise, they also possessed a fighter pilot instinct. But there was another more pressing reason for their extraordinary accomplishments—these were men who had witnessed the merciless brutality of jack-booted Germans as they bombed and shot innocent Poles during the invasion and subsequent occupation of their native land. Some had also witnessed the Russians do likewise. They had waited a long time to be given a decent weapon and a means to fight their murderous adversary. They were determined to make the most of every second in aerial combat. Furthermore, they were quick to admonish British or Commonwealth pilots who showed any form of leniency toward the enemy. As Johnny Kent recalled:

The Poles were fed up with me when I admitted that I could not bring myself to shoot the chap in the parachute and they reminded me of events earlier in the month when we were told that one or two pilots of No. 1 Squadron had baled-out and had then been shot by German fighters. At the time the Poles had asked me if it was true that this was happening. I had to tell them that as far as I knew, it was, at which they asked, 'Oh can we?' I explained that, distasteful as it was, the Germans were within their rights in shooting down our pilots over this country and that, if one of us shot down a German aircraft over France and the pilot bailed out, then we were quite entitled to shoot him. But this was not so over England as, aside from anything else, he would be out of the war and might even be a very useful source of information for us. They thought about this for a bit and then said: 'Yes, we understand—but what if he is over the Channel?' To which I jokingly replied: 'Well you can't let the poor bugger drown can you?' This remark was quite seriously thrown in my teeth when they heard about the 109 pilot I had just shot down. There was no doubt about it, the Poles were playing the game for keeps far more than we were.[20]

This view was echoed by Air Chief Marshall Sir Keith Park:

Their fighting spirit became legendary even among so brave a band of men as the British fighter pilots. The Poles fought with reckless abandon because their cause was to revenge the brutal destruction of their homeland by the armoured divisions and Stuka dive-bombers of Germany.[21]

There was no doubt however, that Poles respected their British counterparts. By this stage Johnny Kent had been nicknamed Kentowski by members of his Polish Squadron, and he was sorry to leave them when he was promoted to take command of 92 Squadron at Biggin Hill:

Before I left, the Squadron gave me a most magnificent party in the Mess at Leconfield and, at the same time, they informed me that I had been awarded a Polish decoration; they presented me with the ribbon of the Krzyz Walecznych and insisted that I have it sewn on my tunic immediately. The party was quite fantastic, but I managed to hold my own and at three o' clock in the morning the only two left on their feet were Johnny Zumbach, my number two, and myself—and I saw him to bed! This feat boosted my reputation with the Poles quite considerably.[22]

In the autumn of 1940 Poles were honoured wherever they went, and the British people took them to their hearts. In restaurants and bars, they were rarely required to pay for their drinks or food, as a grateful public stepped in to foot their bills. Stories of their heroic exploits were broadcast across the radio waves, and journalists clamoured to highlight their exceptional courage. As their fame grew, they were afforded celebrity status, with American journalist

Quentin Reynolds describing them as glamour fighter boys. Nine of 303 Squadron's pilots had become flying aces (indicating they had shot down five or more enemy aircraft), and on 15th December four of them were awarded the Distinguished Flying Cross: Flying Officer Witold Urbanowicz, Pilot Officer Jan Zumbach, Pilot Officer Mirosław Ferić and Flying Officer Zdzisław Henneberg.[23]

Clearly there was a general realisation that Poles had entered the Battle of Britain at a decisive moment in British history and made a huge contribution in the defence of Britain. For their part, Polish pilots were very appreciative of this public recognition, but they also realized that the war had yet to be won. Motivated by a ruthless hatred of the enemy, their thoughts were never far away from their native Poland.

Above: Members of Polish 303 Squadron with the number of enemy aircraft destroyed recorded on one of their planes.

Chapter 5
The Blitz

The blitz of major British cities which began in the September of 1940 continued relentlessly through the autumn and winter months. By the middle of November thirteen thousand tons of high explosives and almost a thousand incendiaries had been dropped on London. Other major cities also received a pounding from the Luftwaffe, particularly those involved with aircraft production. Industrial production centres in Birmingham and Coventry for instance, were an obvious target. Factories in nearby Castle Bromwich were churning out at least three hundred Spitfires and twenty Lancaster bombers a month. Furthermore, vehicle parts, industrial tools, radio components, bombs, shell casings, rifles and a myriad of small arms were manufactured in the area. It was no surprise therefore that Birmingham was the second most heavily bombed city. Bristol was also a prime target because of its importance to aircraft production. Other targets included vital military bases such as the Royal Navy facilities and Marine Barracks at Plymouth. Speaking in October 1940 Goering assured his commanders that Britain was almost on its knees and would soon be begging to surrender.

Encouraged by Goering's misplaced confidence on 28th October at 3. am Germany's ally Italy decided to embark on their own expansionist policy, by issuing an ultimatum to the Greek Prime Minister. Mussolini requested permission to invade Greece unopposed or he would declare war on the Greek people. General Metaxas simply replied, 'Then it is war.' Greece was a valued British ally and had permitted the Royal Navy access to ports in the Mediterranean. On 9th November Churchill gave a speech at London Mansion House:

There is one heroic country to whom our thoughts today go out in new sympathy and admiration. To the valiant Greek people and their armies, now defending their native soil from the latest Italian outrage—to them we send from the heart of old London our faithful promise that amid all our burdens and anxieties we will do our best to aid them in their struggle, and we will never cease to strike at the foul aggressor in ever increasing strength from this time forth until the crimes and treacheries which hang around the neck of

Mussolini, and disgrace the Italian name have been brought to condign and exemplary justice.[1]

However, providing military support for Greece stretched British forces who were beginning a long struggle for control of North Africa and the Middle East. RAF Squadrons were doing their utmost to protect British cities and industrial complexes, but shorter days and longer nights favoured incoming German bombers. Coventry was virtually obliterated on the night of 14th November when bombing continued throughout the night, destroying the medieval centre and ancient Cathedral. While on Sunday 24th November most of the medieval area of Bristol was devastated. The severity of this raid prompted the vicar of St Peters Church to solemnly announce to his congregation that they would probably all die that night. He then proceeded to continue with his evensong service as the Luftwaffe roared overhead.[2]

London, as ever, continued to be pounded on a nightly basis. Polish pilot Bolesław Drobiński paid tribute to Londoners who endured enemy raids:

I admired the population of Londoners. You could see broken shop windows with goods displayed, and a notice on a piece of glass saying business as usual. That spirit you could not break uplifted people. This was in their character.[3]

Defending cities from enemy night raids was a difficult task. Spitfires and Hurricanes which were adept at intercepting daylight attacks were less versatile at night. Over seven divisions of anti-aircraft artillery, barrage balloons and searchlights offered limited protection, but the bombers still reached their targets. Nevertheless, there were RAF successes and injured German pilots shot down over the channel or urban areas often found themselves in the ironic position of lying in city hospitals contemplating the fact that as the Luftwaffe bombers droned overhead they could very well be killed by their own countrymen. German patients were frequently aggressive towards nurses who tried to care for them and exhibited disgusting behaviour. Some deliberately defecated or urinated in their beds. Others pulled out intravenous drips and wound drains. Within professional nursing circles there were debates as to how best to deal with such truculence:

The Sunday Chronicle reported recently that a nurse had been spat upon by a German prisoner and did the right thing in walking away and ignoring the

Left: German Heinkel III bomber over London. Below is the River Thames and Tower Bridge (German photograph)

***Above:** Firefighters in the Blitz.*

insult. From the correspondence to which this gross but characteristic conduct gave rise this opinion was not unanimously approved. Mrs A Townsend, of Bridlington, York, wrote:

> *I should have slapped his face very good and hard.' That is the Yorkshire way, straight from the shoulder and make no mistake about it. We nurses however, approve of our colleagues' dignified conduct, but the less we are called upon to associate with these barbarians the better.[4]*

German pilots were often nursed in the same wards as their victims and while nurses maintained a dignified approach to their care their patients were not so restrained. With shouts of 'cut his bleeding throat nurse' every time a nurse disappeared behind a screen to attend to a German, and other instructions of an abusive nature, nursing the enemy remained a tiresome challenge.

Moreover, the task of defending British cities became increasingly difficult because of deteriorating weather conditions from October onward. This situation also caused problems for members of Bomber Command, who were conducting bombing sweeps against German barges, shipping, docks and industrial areas. Combat reports for 300 Squadron stated that on 10th October 1940:

> *Sgt. Ratajczak, P/O Pluta and Sgt. Gędziorowski took off at 18.35 hrs. First run—12,000 feet to 8,000 feet 4 x 250lb bombs on S.E. Quay. Second run 2 x 250lb bombs on No. 6 basin. Landed in Grantham at 2200 hrs because of navigational difficulties.*

> *Sgt. Kazimierczak, Sgt Sobieszczuk and Sgt. Szmajdowicz took off at 18.39 hrs. Bombed in stick N.W. to S.E. along northern edge of No. 2 basin, 6 x 250lb bombs at 10,000 feet, two bursts observed. Landed at Bodney due to engine failure. Returned to Swinderby 09.30 hrs on 11.10.40.*

On 13th October 1940:

> *F/O Gębicki, Sgt. Hloreme and Sgt. Egierski took off at 17.40 hrs. This aircraft crashed at Oxton near Nottingham. Aircraft burnt out and all crew killed.*

> *Sgt Koczwarski F/O Szponarowicz and Sgt. Satul took off at 17.47 hrs, 4 x 250lb bombs E. to W. of Nos. 6-7 basin. Aircraft crashed at Sherwood near Nottingham. No-one injured in the crash.*[5]

Numbers of fatalities in Bomber Command were much higher than in any other RAF Command and by this stage, one in twenty bomber pilots failed to return from their missions.

November and December 1940 were characterized by intense German bombardments on Hull, Newcastle, Liverpool, Manchester, Glasgow, Plymouth and Cardiff. On 29th December London experienced one of the fiercest nights of the blitz. Referred to by Londoners as the Second Great Fire of London, this terrifying attack inflicted severe damage to hospitals, churches, municipal buildings and the city's general infrastructure. Mr Walter Bentley resident engineer of St Guy's hospital described the attack:

Above: ***Planes supplied under U.S Lend-Lease agreement.***

An odd thing followed the first bomb as the switchboard main breakers were thrown in not out as you might expect. This put on all the lights. There was a frantic rush to the generating station. To have all the lights on with the enemy overhead was clearly not desirable. Though the skies were lit up by incendiaries anyway. Very soon a high explosive fell on the hospital hitting one of the oldest buildings—Dorcas ward, part of the original Guys building in 1725. The Martha ward heaved up. All patients were in the basement and no-one was hurt. Further bomb blasts followed. Fires increased in intensity. Police requested evacuation of the hospital but only two roads were open to ambulances and one might be closed by fire at any moment. Steps were taken at once to carry patients to a rest centre outside the zone of fire. Students worked like galley slaves, wrapping up sick people and carrying them to ambulances which the police provided. Some nurses went with patients. Others remained behind. Casualties not coming in because approach to hospital too difficult. Then worst of troubles began. The wind changed and freshened as it did so. Before we knew what was happening, over the flaming area outside our walls the whole park and hospital were obliterated by a snowstorm of fire sparks. I don't know how else to describe it. They were so thick and constant that any man who had gone out without his tin hat would have had his hair catch fire. Then a miracle happened! When things looked at their worst, the wind veered round once more, and it began to rain. All clear sounded. Then a new fire on roof of Hunts House and a hard fight to put it out. Everything finally settled by 3.am on 30th December.[6]

As 1940 drew to a close British, Polish and Commonwealth forces were still holding their own against Axis powers. For a considerable time, British troops had been involved in a cat and mouse game with the Germans and Italians across the expansive deserts of North Africa and the Middle East. By the end of December, three Italian camps were destroyed and over 40,000 prisoners taken. The Italians were also under siege in Greece, where they were meeting firm resistance. But there was little respite for the Allies as German forces launched a counteroffensive in North Africa. In the United States President Roosevelt did sign a Lend-Lease Bill which offered some financial support for Britain's war effort, but on the home front prolonged raids were taking a toll on the health and wellbeing of ordinary civilians. The bitter winter was followed by a cold

and frosty spring and the relentless symphony of war threatened to undermine morale. Determined to improve ground defences the government substantially increased the number of search lights and anti-aircraft weaponry. This policy had some impact. German losses amounted to twenty-eight in January, but this figure had risen to one hundred and twenty-four by

Left: U.S. Lend-Lease Howitzers.

May. Improvements were made in radar assisted RAF night flights and Bristol Beaufighters were eventually fitted with their own radar systems.

Regardless of increased German losses Goering remained convinced that Britain could be bombed into submission, and on 10th May 1941 London experienced a night of bombing so fearful and extensive that it overshadowed all previous raids. Guided by a full moon, Luftwaffe bombers descended on the city just after 11pm and dropped a total of seven hundred and eleven tons of high explosives and eighty-six thousand, one hundred and seventy-three incendiaries. Firefighters were forced to deal with over two thousand major fires and seven hundred acres of land was destroyed. Some of the German pilots flew three sorties during this dreadful night and bombing of the capital was relentless until nearly 6.am. In response to these incoming raids Fighter Command deployed three hundred and twenty-five pilots across the country including twenty-four long range fighters. They claimed twenty-eight enemy aircraft. Yet despite their concerted efforts nearly one thousand five hundred Londoners were killed on this night, and almost two thousand injured. The Houses of Parliament, Westminster Abbey, the British Museum and five hospitals had been bombed. Government propaganda films assured the population that 'Britain can take it,' but after months of continued bombing Londoners were heartily 'sick of taking it,' and there were growing demands to start 'giving it back.' Eventually therefore, the Ministry of Information dropped 'Britain can take it' films because they were deemed to be defeatist. Fortunately, towards the end of May, enemy raids lessened in frequency and intensity; primarily because Hitler was forced to divert some of his aircraft to assist the shambolic Italians in their efforts to conquer Greece.

RAF Fighter and Bomber Commands meanwhile worked strenuously in defence of the realm and vigilantly patrolled the channel for enemy formations. A 306 Squadron report dated 17th June 1941 summarized the day's events:

Twelve Hurricanes II, 306 Polish Squadron took off from North Weald at 18.45 hrs to rendezvous over Southend with eighteen Blenheims and 242 and 56 Squadrons at 8,000ft and act as close escort to the bombers during an attack near Bethune. They crossed the French coast at 12,000ft and were attacked from below and ahead by 3 Me's which approached to within 500 yards and then passed under the whole formation and attacked from astern. After the bombing they were attacked by 7-9 Me's singly from the beam and astern, and by 1 Me from

Above: *German bombing raid on London with iconic Tower Bridge in the distance.*

ahead. Numerous combats developed, but all the results could not be observed, as the pilots had to maintain contact with the bombers. But F/O Słońsk destroyed 1 Me. 109, which he saw crash in a field. Sgt Jeka destroyed 1 Me. 109, the pilot of which he and others of the Squadron saw bale out. Sgt. Kosmowski probably destroyed 1 Me. which he attacked from 150 yards and from which he and Sgt Otto Pudrycki saw white smoke coming and F/O Zielinski confirms this. F/O Tielinski attacked 2 Me. 109's, one with two short bursts at 100 yards and one with two long bursts at 150 yards. In each case he saw his bullets entering enemy aircraft but had to break off contact to re-join his Squadron before he could observe results. No claim made. F/Lt. Zaremba saw bomb bursts and fires amongst the buildings attacked, but again observation was difficult because of continuous fighting. On the return journey, the Squadron was continuously attacked by Me.'s which followed them to Mid-Channel. Over the Channel, Sgt. Kosmowski attacked one Me. at 300 yards, closing to 50 yards, and saw it dive absolutely vertically, apparently out of control at 2,000 feet. This was seen by S/Ldr. Rolski, who had warned him of the presence of the enemy aircraft. This is claimed as destroyed. Six more pilots had combats but could not follow them up and observe results. Weather was excellent with no cloud and excellent visibility. All the Me's had the engines painted yellow from the cockpit forward. Rounds of ammunition fired:

S/L. Rolski 40 x 12 M.G. Sgt. Jeka 100 x 12 M.G. F/O Zielinski 150 x 12 M.G. Sgt Kosmowski 100 x 8 M.G. F/O Rutkowski 150 x 12 M.G. Sgt. Pudrycki did not fire, F/O Zaremba 150 x 12 M.G. Sgt. Machowiak 10 x 12 M.G. F/O Słońsk 320 x 8 M.G. P/O Skalski did not fire, P/O Langhamer 20 x 8 M.G. Sgt. Pietrzak 100 x 12 M.G.[7]

There were no pilot casualties on this mission. A report from 303 Squadron dated 18th June 1941 also reported some success:

Above: *Henryk Pietrzak celebrating after shooting down 500th enemy aircraft for Polish Air Force.*

Twelve Spitfire 11B 303 Polish Squadron left Marston at 1735hrs after 145 Squadron and rendezvoused over Marston with two Hurricane Squadrons, and over Hastings with bombers and escort at 19,000 feet. Course Dungeness Boulogne and target area. Kept visual touch with Spitfires below. North East of target area, experienced first attack by about twelve Me. 109's. A.A. (anti-aircraft fire) was very strong, but rather erratic at this point. The fighting developed near St. Inglevert, and both 303 and Spitfire Squadron below were attacked. Messerschmitts appeared to be flying in ones, twos, threes and fours. Messerschmitts attacked the Squadron which was flying in fours from above and from the beam. Between Calais and Cap Gris Nez S/Ldr. Lapkowski saw four Me. 109's (possibly Five) above and climbing to the port side, selected one of the enemy aircraft. He attacked it from out of the sun, and from astern and gave a short burst from cannon and machine guns from 200/50 yards, upon which the enemy aircraft developed a little smoke and then burst into flames and crashed inside the French coast. He made a further attack on one of another formation of four Me. 109's, probably F. at 17/18,000 feet making no claim.

F/O Łokuciewski as No. 2 to S/Ldr Łapkowski climbed to the starboard side and selected another Me. 109F from the same formation of four. The enemy aircraft dived together with another Me.109 and our pilot followed them, then selected one and after he had dived below the enemy aircraft pulled his nose up sharply, and fired a short burst from cannon and machine guns from 30 yards range into the middle of enemy aircraft. There was a large cloud of black smoke and a large piece of the aircraft was seen to fall off. The enemy aircraft rolled over in flames over France out of sight. P/O Drobiński was flying in the same formation of four as the Squadron Leader, but did not share in the attack in the above mentioned, Me. 109's. He then saw two Me. 109's in line astern going to attack two Spitfires below. He turned sharp to starboard and attacked one of these enemy aircraft giving it a short burst from 5/600 yards to frighten him off. He then closed in and from above and astern gave another short burst at 400 yards. Smoke and flames appeared immediately, and the enemy aircraft went down which is confirmed by Sgt. Palak. He then turned left and saw three or four Me. 109's above and behind. The pilot was then at about 15,600 feet but A.A. fire prevented him from making an attack. He turned west

Right: Garden cultivated on a bomb crater.

climbing and joined two
aircraft of his Squadron, and
then noticed two aircraft
flying towards France below,
and recognised them as Me.
109E. He dived and fired a
short burst from cannon and
machine guns from 50 yards
from below and astern.
Black smoke and flames
appeared, and two pilots of the Squadron saw this enemy aircraft crash
into the sea. P/O Drobiński then had to take evasive action as the
second Me. 109 was trying to attack him, but then dived away.
Ammunition fired F/O Łokuciewski 3 rounds cannon, 24 rounds m. g.
each gun. S/Ldr. Łapkowski 5 rounds cannon, 30 rounds m. g. each
gun. F/O Drobiński 45 rounds cannon, 180 rounds m. g. each gun.
Enemy casualties casualties 2 Me. 109F destroyed and 2 Me. 109E
destroyed. **Our casualties** Nil.[8] 12 aircraft landed at Northolt 19.20 hrs.

On the 22nd June 1941 Mirosław Ferić flying between Hazebrook and the
French coast reported:

Just after leaving the target area, I saw a single Me. 109E climbing up
to attack the Squadron. I turned down to him sharply and checked his
climb by a short burst from 300 yards, but I got into a spin which I
corrected quickly and luckily found the 109 in my sights as I came out
of the spin. I got to within 150 yards and gave him another burst
whereupon I saw large pieces of break away from the enemy aircraft
and saw it crash 7 or 8 miles north of Hazebrook.[9]

A few days later Ferić noted:

Near Calais my Squadron Leader gave the order for a low-level attack
on an aerodrome, probably Coqualles. We dived and saw about 8 Me.
109's dispersed on the ground. I fired my cannons and m/g's at one of
these enemy aircraft and am sure I damaged it. I fired 32 rounds from
each of 2 cannons and 70 rounds from each of 4 m/g's.[10]

By now, Polish Squadrons had gained a solid reputation for their incredible visual awareness, and decisive quick thinking. Bob Nawarski recalled:

The Germans could be quite cocky, but you knew how to evaluate a chap, or at least you thought you knew what a chap could do or not do. You had to concentrate on where he was, or it could be the end of you. The more experience you had the wiser you were. I could actually spot enemy planes before anyone else and notified the leader, that was the pattern on several occasions. You thought you could go on forever, but a very good friend of mine was shot down and I never saw him again.[11]

Kazimierz Budzik described his thoughts just before engaging the enemy:

The spirit in the Squadron was tremendous. You are in this echelon and personally before going into battle just above my heel used to tremble—just before diving. But in the actual dive fear was gone. You needed to concentrate on the cannons and machine guns, and you had no fear all the while you were doing this. We used to forget easily when we got back—played some cards and had a drink. The majority of pilots were very easy going.[12]

On the home front, as spring turned to summer, seemingly in defiance of the terrifying horrors of bombing, hospital records revealed that Britons were getting fitter and healthier. The extension of free school meals and milk for children, subsidised British canteens for the workforce and widespread vaccination programmes had combined to shore up the nation's health. Elsewhere, British forces had withdrawn from Crete and were mounting a strong counteroffensive against German troops in North Africa. Although the success of desert warfare was largely dependent on the outcome of sea warfare, because most of the supplies to British troops in this area were shipped across the Mediterranean. Hitler, meanwhile, committed a massive strategic error. Heavily influenced by a long-standing racial ideology, which foolishly asserted that German Teutons would always be victorious over Slavic races, he chose to invade Soviet Russia on 22nd June 1941. Code-named Operation Barbarossa the invasion was a flagrant breach of the Nazi-Soviet non-aggression pact he had earlier signed with Stalin, and effectively signalled the beginning of the end for German forces. In a repetition of Napoleon's disastrous Russian campaign of 1812, Hitler's Nazis were subsequently trapped in the sub-zero temperatures of a severe Russian winter.

Chapter 6
The Ground Crew

The Battle of Britain and all subsequent victorious aerial combat during the war was won in part because of ground crew expertise. Working tirelessly behind the scenes in aircraft hangars and RAF installations across the country members of the ground crew ensured that planes were maintained in good order and repaired as quickly as possible when necessary. Pilots lives depended on the technical skill and dedication of mechanics, engineers, and armaments experts. As pilot Bob Nawarski, who flew with 303, 302 and 316 Squadrons, explained:

The Squadron might have twenty-five or thirty aircraft, but the mechanics always had the aircraft prepared for you. They would check the petrol tank was full, ammunition was full, controls were checked, and they made sure radio was working. We always found without exception that they were always very good. If they said it was working, you knew it would be. You wouldn't suddenly take off and find you didn't have enough petrol. Pre-flight checks were all done for you. When you yourself got in you would test the radio because earpieces were in the helmet you see. The altimeter would be at zero. Squadron would taxi the take off in sections of two, one slightly behind the other. Squadron leader would take off first with wingman, then make a circuit, then we all joined up and flew in the direction we needed to go. You were very well protected in a Spitfire. There was armour plating from behind, to protect the back of your head, and nothing could really get to you sideways. The enemy would have to be very lucky to get you in the right place. But after a fight you didn't know the damage until you came back and noticed you had some holes.[1]

The wartime journalist Arkady Fiedler writing in 1943 documented the situation faced by 303 Squadron mechanics at the end of 15th September 1940:

Left: *Flt.Sgt. Mieczysław Popek with ground crew.*

Right: Artwork including photographs of 307 Squadron ground crew.

MECHANICY DYWIZJONU.

„MERLIN"

At the end of the victorious day the Squadron's Hurricanes were in a piteous condition. They had sustained all sorts of damage, control fins shot away, radiators smashed, control cables cut, wings and shields riddled, even propellers had had a bad time. One machine had the main wing spar nearly broken at the junction with the fuselage. The damage was clearly beyond the resources of the Squadron's repair shop. Yet the mechanics did not lose heart. It was expected that the enemy would return the next day in greater force than ever. The mechanics realized how much depended on them now. They went to work and worked all night without being ordered: at such times orders are superfluous. It was not merely a matter of their personal ambition but of the Squadron's very existence. They were exalted by an inspired frenzy; their fingers were winged; and they triumphed. The incredible, the impossible was achieved; at the dawn of 16th September there were again twelve fighters ready to take off. The day of glory for British and Polish fighters had brought a night of glory for Polish mechanics. Lieutenant Wiórkiewicz has all the qualities to inspire others—and he does inspire them. It is difficult to estimate the services Wiórkiewicz has rendered to Squadron 303; they are beyond all powers of appreciation. It is impossible to think of the victorious 303 without him and his staff of mechanics.[2]

Engineering officers tended to their aircraft as though they were their 'babies' or 'darlings.' They were meticulous with every detail and highly respected by their peers. Often working through the night to repair damaged planes mechanics were the unsung heroes of the RAF and PAF. Flying Officer for 303

Squadron Wacław Wiórkiewicz described his approach to his work:

An aircraft is a living creature, that consists of particular systems, blood, nerves, nervous system, gasoline, hydraulics, compressed air, radio, oxygen, armament, aircraft instruments—all this is full of life and works together for the common effort—combat flight. Each of these circuits requires its doctor, when one doctor works on the radio but the fuel system or armament are not his speciality, he does not even touch it, as he knows that he could damage it instantly. The modern Hurricane is purebred and requires caring care. In their job, mechanics like their own aircraft. Polish traditions and habits come out. It was tradition that each aircraft had its own overseer and assistant—they did not like others and did not want them. Initially, when we blindly followed the English rituals, and did not follow our customs, it was happening that, as in the bible, various doctors-mechanics argued for a long time on methods of repairing an ill aircraft. Return to the Polish norms left an aircraft with constant carers, sensitive, tender for the smallest defect of their own aircraft.[3]

Above: *Ground crew checking propeller.*

Above: Missile production.

Even on occasions when Polish mechanics were disappointed with the type of aircraft they were required to service, they stoically ploughed on regardless. Flight Lieutenant Hale, Adjutant of 307 Squadron noted:

I remember with what consternation the pilots discovered that the Squadron was to be equipped with Defiants and not front gun fighters. After the first shock had worn off there was a fine spirit of determination to make the best of these aircraft and to become operational as rapidly as possible.[4]

This determination was finally rewarded, and the ground crew of 307 Squadron gave a huge sigh of relief when they were eventually equipped with Beaufighters II in August 1941 and Beaufighters VI in May 1942. They visited the factory where the aircraft were produced and wrote a warm heartfelt letter of thanks to the designers and assembly workers. Indeed, an inscribed copy of the Polish night fighter song was presented to George White, the founder of Bristol Aeroplane Company at Filton, where the aircraft were made.[5]

Ground crew empathy with their aircraft naturally extended to empathy with their pilots, some of whom took various lucky mascots into battle. Most of these tended to be fluffy toys received as gifts from loved ones. Others were given religious symbols in the hope that these would provide in-flight protection. Squadron Leader Franciszek Kornicki for example, always flew with two crucifixes, which were attached in his Spitfire cockpit by his rigger and fitter. In the build up to battles spiritual sustenance was very important to the Poles as Kazimierz Budzik recalled:

Before battles a priest used to come to see if you wanted to take Holy Communion. People used to be killed of course, so I used to go and take Communion. I don't know anyone who used drugs—definitely not! But we had lots of cigarettes and chewing gum. Sometimes after battle I'd go for a drink and then have a good sleep.[6]

There was a symbiotic camaraderie and affection between pilots and ground crew—a recognition that everyone had their part to play in winning the war. This relationship extended to their social and community living. Ground crew also included medical and catering staff. Bob Nawarski described his memories fondly:

The food was good. If anything, we were pampered. Nutritionally they made sure we had all the nutrients and vitamins. I felt a bit guilty actually because I had oranges and bananas. We had them because we were operational pilots. The Sergeants Mess had cheap drinks I know that! If you were likely to fly the next day you didn't drink too much. Most of us were quite aware we had a responsibility to each other. We played snooker and tennis. I was quite good at snooker at one stage. Our pub was the 'Orchard,' its still there. Atmosphere was quite nice and the chap who owned it was nice. If the Squadron had some success that day, he would produce drinks on the house. We had a very friendly reception.[7]

According to the memoirs of ground crew, mechanics, engineers, riggers, fitters and armourers were often required to work around the clock during periods of intense activity. Their day usually began at 4.30 am and they were expected to be present and correct, ready for duty in their hangars at 5.30 am. The daily routine for an armourer started with an inspection of aircraft. Firstly, he would take off the fourteen access panels, unload the eight guns and thoroughly clean them with flannelette and a rod. Other pieces of flannelette were then used to clean the gunsight lens and reflector glass. The trolley accumulator, which was used to turn over aircraft engines, was plugged into an electric socket and switched on. Next the armourer would go under the starboard wheel bay to set weapons from Safe and Fire, to Safe to Fire. Once the aircraft took off the disabling switch closed, enabling guns to be fired. In order to test guns on the ground an override switch was fitted to the starboard wheel bay. Following on from this the armourer would test gun sight and all functions. Cleaning the reflector glass was also extremely important, since no armourer wanted his pilot to go chasing a speck of dirt on the reflector glass all the way to Pas de Calais. Gun sight was then switched off. Safety ring on pilot's firing button was turned from Safe to Fire and button pressed while listening for breech blocks to clang forward, then safety ring turned back to safe. Filament was removed from gun sight once cooled down and replaced with spare filament from filament holder next to gun sight, and original filament fitted in holder—test gun sight again. Armourer would then

Above Production of aircraft tyres.

swing down to the ground to set Safe/Fire switch back to safe. Using a special feeler gauge, he would ensure that all breech blocks were forward, and all firing pins released. Guns were then re-loaded and access panels replaced. The aircraft-log book (form 700) was then signed to indicate inspection was complete.[8]

Once the pilot was safely strapped in his cockpit with his helmet secured, he signalled to the ground crew that he was ready to start the engine. When the Merlin engine was running smoothly the pilot switched power from external to internal control. Ground crew always watched aircraft take off before coiling up cable of accumulator trolley and parking it out of the way. They then prepared further ammunition ready to re-arm—this process could take as little as twenty minutes.[9]

In addition to armourers there were riggers and fitters who serviced instruments and frames, mechanics who ensured engines were well maintained and R/T fitters who repaired radios and electrical circuits. Much of the mechanical and electrical work was performed by women. The British Women's Auxiliary Air Force (WAAF) was established in 1939 and included over 183,317 volunteers. A further 33,932 women joined in response to the call-up of 1941 and the WAAF became an integral part of the Armed Forces. Despite this increase in number however, there was a shortage of ground support staff, and yet again, assisted by world events, a timely infusion of Poles arrived to swell the ranks. Germany's implementation of Operation Barbarossa prompted the release of thousands of Polish families from brutal, bleak Soviet prison camps, because they were now required to fight a common enemy. Overnight, Russia became a British ally and Polish refugees, many of them orphaned children, made their way to British held territories in the Middle East. Senior Polish military leaders were authorized to establish a Polish army in exile, with the aim of joining forces with Allied military personnel. Inspired and led by leaders such as General Anders, Polish men and women journeyed across the expanse of Russia and gathered on the eastern shores of the Caspian Sea, awaiting transport to Persia. Some had travelled for months in appalling conditions. By roads in spartan lorries, by rail in cargo trains, or simply on foot they endeavoured to find new avenues from which to fight. Many young boys became trapped in collective small holdings in south Russia, other refugees succumbed to starvation or freezing temperatures and died along the way. Eventually Polish officers formed food distribution stations along the 4,000-kilometre route, but this only consisted of small amounts of flour and fat. Gradually more and more refugees arrived at Port Krasnovodsk. They then boarded the Molotow tanker and sailed to Pahlavi in Iran. Here, British forces assumed control of Polish families and most were moved to Palestine following a six-week quarantine period.[10] By 10th November 1942 they were housed at Qastina and military schools were established. Further camps were formed in Te-el-Kebir and Heliopolis in Egypt, some families were scattered as far away as Mombassa and Karachi. Teresa Babicz travelled by train to Krasnovodsk in Kazakhstan. From there she was sent to India with approximately five thousand women and children. Eventually she arrived in England:

I was taught by Miss Wood at Grendon Hall near Aylesbury. Her fiancé was a Polish pilot who died in the Battle of Britain. She made a vow to dedicate her professional life to teaching Polish children. [11]

By this point hundreds of previously interned Poles had managed to journey to England.[12] The British Air Ministry and Ministry of Defence had proposed the formation of a Polish WAAF (PLSK) in 1942 and six hundred young Polish women, eager to help the war effort, volunteered to join up.[13] The following year they were permitted to wear the Polish crowned Eagle insignia on their uniforms.

Those who trained as officers were usually assigned positions in intelligence units, code and cipher groups, air traffic control, scientific development, photographic research, meteorology, administrative and accounting departments, or within technical instructions fields. Non-commissioned officers often became nursing or dental orderlies, plotters or watchers in operations room, clerks, parachute packers, telephonists, catering staff, storekeepers, or mechanics. By 1943, members of PLSK served in twenty-six RAF stations and accounted for approximately thirteen per cent of RAF ground support.[14] In this same year the Air Ministry introduced a Polish aircraft apprentices training scheme.[15] Officers serving with the PAF scoured Middle Eastern refugee camps looking for suitable apprenticeship candidates. But although there were at least three thousand boys and nearly seven hundred girls in the camps at this stage, it became clear that boys without any form of documentation would lie about their age in the hope of being accepted for training. Malnutrition and effects of their previous internments had stunted their growth and made age assessments more difficult. The required age for apprenticeship was fifteen and a half years.

After much deliberation two hundred and sixty-four boys from various camp locations were chosen for training at RAF Halton. They assembled at Al Hamra, travelled to Fayid, then on to Suez where they boarded the liner Mauritania. Their journey took them round the coast of Africa before arriving in Liverpool on 14th August 1943. A further cohort of boys travelled aboard troop ship Strathmore, sailing through the Mediterranean, reaching Liverpool in December 1943.[16]

Upon arrival at Halton these young Polish recruits were given serial numbers between 709001 and 709307. They were kitted out with new underwear and

Above: Flt Lt Stanislaw Socha with Sergeant Jan Hrunyk.

RAF blue serge uniforms and given the sum of ten shillings. In addition to Polish insignia displayed on caps and side hats they also wore an apprentice badge which consisted of a four-blade propeller set in an annulus, on their left sleeve. The word Poland was attached just below the shoulder seam and a red cap band completed the outfit. Depending on requirements the number of Polish apprentices fluctuated. For instance, one hundred boys left Halton to undertake training at No.1 radio school on 4th January Cranwell but twenty-nine more arrived from the Middle East two days later. Lady Jersey was appointed

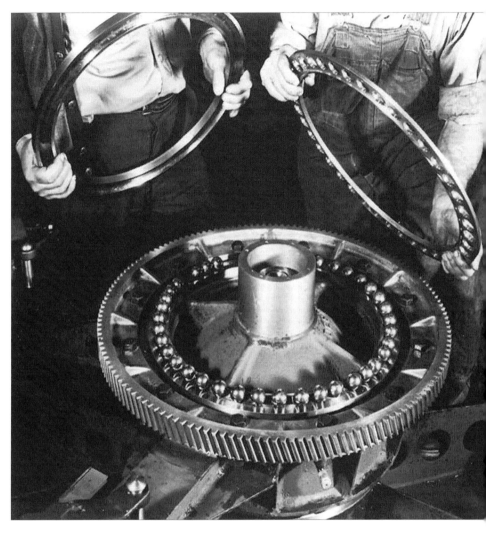

Above: *U.S. munitions production plant.*

Honorary Guardian of these young recruits and during the summer and Christmas vacation periods over three hundred English families opened their doors to welcome them. The Irish Red Cross also invited one hundred and fifty-six boys to spend holidays in Ireland.[17]

By 1944 RAF ground support included members from forty-eight nationalities. During the Battle of Britain period alone three hundred and twelve ground crew members were killed and four hundred and sixty- seven injured. Luftwaffe attacks on Biggin Hill and other southern airfields exacted a heavy toll on personnel, since much of the repair work on damaged aircraft took place on open dispersals rather than in hangars, due to shortage of space in the latter. Although the only ground crew member of 303 Squadron to be killed by enemy action was Aircraftsman Antoni Rossochacki.[18] Dangers of working on operational airfields also included working with live explosives and highly flammable material. Often accidents occurred due to extreme fatigue. For example, there were incidents where aircraftsmen walked into working propellers, fell off scaffolding or injured themselves with sharp tools. These were more common during winter months because of additional hazards caused by frost and snow. Polish ground crew however were more accustomed to lower temperatures, and consequently had less weather-related accidents.

Senior British pilots paid tribute to the high standard of professionalism exhibited by the Polish 303 Squadron ground crew stating:

We must never forget how, in the days of the Battle of Britain the ground staff of the Squadron worked strenuously and without a word of complaint under difficult conditions. There was one period over three weeks in which work continued for twenty-four hours a day, the airmen sleeping on the floors of huts, snatching hasty meals between long intervals servicing the machines which did such marvellous damage to the vaunted Luftwaffe. On one occasion three aircraft only out of a flight of twelve returned serviceable from an operation, and by the following morning the nine damaged aircraft were ready once more for another attack. The few English mechanics who worked with the Squadron were amazed at the quickness of the Poles in adopting themselves to English methods and English machines.[19]

Polish ground crew were adept at applying skilled knowledge speedily and accurately. Furthermore, they disseminated this knowledge by means of a variety of publications. In 1940 Wiadomosci ze Swiata (News from the World) a Daily Bulletin of Polish Air Units was published, in 1941 Biuletyn Lotniczy, a Polish Aeronautical Digest was published by N.Pl, RAF Polish Department, and in the same year Mysl Lotnicza was published by the Polish Air Force Headquarters.[20] These publications were supplemented by weekly, fortnightly and monthly periodicals which kept PAF members in touch with other Polish forces. Reports of ground crew staff recorded in logbooks and summaries of workloads highlight their bravery and commitment. As Air Chief Marshall Sir Keith Park vividly recalled:

During the Battle of Britain, I kept my Hurricane at Northolt Aerodrome from which No. 303 Squadron operated daily and, on

*several occasions, I witnessed the fiery spirit of the Poles when ordered
up to intercept the enemy. On other occasions I saw the Polish pilots
landing back from combat and enthusiastically recounting the action.
I was told by my RAF ground crew that on many occasions the Polish
fighters were spattered with the blood of the enemy so close had they
engaged the Germans. It should never be forgotten that this historic
battle could not have been won without the dedication and bravery of
the ground crew (including WAAFs) who serviced the Spitfires and
Hurricanes in spite of the heavy bombings of their aerodromes by day
and often by night.[21]*

In addition to mechanics, riggers, fitters and operations room staff, pilots were
also supported by medical personnel such as Zygmunt Wodecki the doctor
assigned to 303 Squadron. The rapid speed at which aeroplanes on fire hurtled
to the ground produced what became known as airmen's burns.' These burns
caused deep penetration and destruction of body tissue. They were initially
treated with sulphonamide powder and Vaseline gauze, or tannic acid, until a
pioneering surgeon named Archibald McIndoe devised new treatments. Tulle
gras dressings were introduced and affected limbs suspended in saline bags to
aid healing. McIndoe established his 'Guinea Pig' unit at Queen Victoria
Hospital East Grinstead, where he concentrated on the psychological and
physical well-being of his patients. In cases where men's faces had been burned
away, surgeons operated in stages:

*Over the course of weeks flesh and skin was replaced and noses swung
down in flaps from foreheads, even being so careful as to include a
tiny edge of the hair bearing skin where it would normally meet the
forehead. This was turned around into this new nose to be tucked
inside the nostril so there were hairs in the nostril.[22]*

Furthermore, as Princess Mary's Royal Air Force Nursing Service (PMRAFNS)
sister Monica Baly stressed:

*You had a pressure to get people back to duty, particularly in the Air
Force where you were dealing with people like pilots who were very
valuable and precious. You had to get them back into the air as soon
as possible.[23]*

On a day to day basis medical teams usually attended to minor injuries such as
cuts and grazes and dealt with the occasional concussion case caused by
propellers. They were also responsible for giving inoculations and for
conducting numerous medical experiments designed to improve pilot safety.

Below: Eleanor Roosevelt, wife of the US President, meeting members of the Women's Auxiliary Air Force.

Above:: Polish Air Force ground crew.

These included measuring combat stress in pilots and gunners, assessing the effectiveness of battledress, and gauging the brain's reaction to low oxygen levels. As Bob Nawarski recalled:

> *At 10,000 feet you could wear normal battledress, higher than that we had big stockings, thick wool ones. They kept you quite warm. We had a sweater underneath and gloves. It was important to know how aircraft behaved when flying low and very high. You were more aware of space flying high. You had to switch oxygen on otherwise you could lose consciousness. It was sinister because you could think you were alright. To drum it into you they put you in a chamber and diminished the oxygen levels while you did tasks. Then they showed you your paper to see how you had done. Later-on you had to put the oxygen on straight away before take-off. We then had special trousers because as you started to dive the more G force (air pressure) would be in your trousers. It would increase and squeeze you. Your eyelids were very much heavier, you just stopped you see. Without a G suit you would black out at four or four and a half G, with a suit you wouldn't black out until nine G.[24]*

Experiments to assess pilot reactions to temperature and atmospheric changes continued throughout the war. These resulted in the introduction of significant safety measures and better training techniques.

The Ground Crew of 303 Squadron

Posted in on 22nd July/2nd August 1940:

F/Lt. W. Żyborski	Adjutant	Cpl. J. Zbrożek	Instr Mkrs
F/Lt. J. Giejsztowt	Intelligence Officer	Cpl. J. Lemański	WEM
		LAC. T Strzeszyński	Elect II
F/O. W. Wiórkiewicz	Engineering Officer	LAC. M. Malinowski	W/Op
		LAC. M. Kobierzycki	Clerk
W/O. K. Mozół	Fitter I	LAC. J. Zgraja	Clerk GD
W/O. A. Mikołajczak	Fitter I	LAC. M. Kowalski	Fl Rigger
F/Sgt. J. Nowacki	Fitter I	LAC. J. Cendrowski	Fl Mechanic
F/Sgt. H Starzyński	Fitter I	LAC. G. Strzępka	Fitter II A
F/Sgt. J. Buśko	WEM	LAC. F. Gurzyński	Fitter II E
Sgt. B. Pianko	Fitter	LAC. J. Komorowski	Fitter II E
Sgt. K. Blachuta	Fitter	LAC. M. Kościelniak	Fitter II E
Sgt. J. Badełek	Fitter	LAC. E. Siemasko	Fl Rigger
Sgt. J. Orczykowski	Fitter	LAC. S. Bochnacki	Fitter II A
Sgt. A. Krzywicki	Fitter	LAC. S. Lotko	Fitter II E
Sgt. J. Mikołajczyk	Fitter	LAC. B. Zaremba	Armourer
Sgt. A. Majcherczyk	Fitter	LAC. M. Gąsowski	Armourer
Sgt. J. Sobek	Armourer	LAC. F. Noculak	Armourer
Sgt. L. Lata	Fitter	LAC. W. Ślęczkowski	Armourer
Sgt. M. Ziarkowski	WEM	LAC. A. Bartczak	Fitter II A
Cpl. R. Frycze	Fitter I	LAC. T. Cedrowski	Fitter II A
Cpl. S. Suwiński	Fitter I	LAC. P. Bieliński	Fitter II A
Cpl. A Leśniewicz	Fitter I	LAC. W. Chmielewski	Fitter II E
Cpl. K. Moczulski	Fitter I	LAC. W. Biernat	Equipment Assistant
Cpl. J. Włodarczyk	Fitter I	LAC. Z. Smolnicki	Fl Mechanic
Cpl. S. Pawlas	Fitter I	LAC. E. Prokop	WEM
Cpl. K. Szrajer	Inst. Rep.	LAC. E. Słapik	WEM
Cpl. B. Janiak	ACH/GD	LAC. W. Nabokoff	Elect II
Cpl. W. Wasiński	Armourer	LAC. T. Białyński	W/Op
Cpl. Z. Ruczka	Armourer	LAC. B. Straszyński	W/Op
Cpl. Z. Sroka	Armourer	AC1. J. Łuszczek	Fl Rigger
Cpl. W. Ławruszczuk	Fitter I	AC1. R. Kwiatkowski	Fl Rigger
Cpl. L. Dzierzbicki	Fitter II A	AC1. S. Zaręba	Fl Rigger
Cpl. W. Roubo	Fitter II	AC1. A. Rossochacki	Fl Mechanic
Cpl. J. Pełka	Fitter II E	AC1. A. Rossochacki	Fl Mechanic
Cpl. T. Żurakowski	Fitter II E	AC1. M. Gadomski	Fl Mechanic
Cpl. J Krakiewic	Equipment Assistant	AC1. M. Lędzki	Fl Mechanic

AC1. E. Karas...................ACH/GD
AC1. J. Sikora..................ACH/GD
AC1. S. Bieniek................ACH/GD
AC1. Z. Kazimierczak.......ACH/GD
AC1. M. Sapeta...............ACH/GD
AC1. B. Kciuk..................Fl Rigger
AC1. S. Chmielewski........Fl Rigger
AC1. S. Makowski............Fl Mechanic
AC1. F. Matuska...............Fl Mechanic
AC1. J. Brycki..................Fl Mechanic
AC1. T. Kwissa.................Fl Mechanic
AC1. A. Kapciak...............ACH/GD
AC1. W. Raczkowski.........ACH/GD
AC1. B. Sikora..................ACH/GD
AC1. R. Czeremański........Armourer
AC1. J. Hering.................Armourer
AC1. I. Włodarczyk.........Armourer
AC1. W. Mądry...............Armourer
AC1. J. Waluga...............Armourer
AC1. F. Kowalczyk...........Armourer
AC1. R. Paradowski.........Armourer
AC1. F. Wolnik.................Armourer
AC1. M. Kady..................Armourer
AC1. M. Karwowski.........Armourer
AC1. T. Borowik...............ACH/GD
AC1. J. Strzelecki.............ACH/GD
AC1. S. Kubiak.................ACH/GD
AC1. W. Gebler...............Elect I
AC1. W. Burdziejów..........Elect II
AC1. M. Bronisz..............Clerk GD
AC1. J. Krawczyk............Equipment
                                          Assistant
AC1. J. Pach...................Armourer
AC2. Z. Gniot
AC2. H. Brudnoch
AC2. M. Kozak
AC2. A. Gulski
AC2. M. Witczak
AC2. C. Bartosiak
AC2. J. Galli
AC2. C. Wyrzykowski

AC2. K. Szczepański
AC2. L. Kubas
AC2. P. Szymański
AC2. S. Ziętarski
AC2. E. Malinowski
AC2. L. Świstuń
AC2. J. Pacek
AC2. S. Karasiński
AC2. J. Krzysztofiński
AC2. H. Pasławski
AC2. W. Kupczynski
AC2. J. Gołowacz
AC2. D. Maj
AC2. J. Rybarczyk
AC2. A. Rogoziński
AC2. H. Zabłocki
AC2. S. Mrowiec
AC2. A. Wala
AC2. C. Maciaszek
AC2. J. Ślusarz
AC2. A. Żyborski

Posted in on 3rd August 1940:

P/O. J. Walters RAF..........Interpreter
P/O. E. H. Hadwen RAF....Intelligence
                                              Officer
F/Sgt. G. L. Quirk RAF
F/Sgt. L. E. king RAF
Sgt. A. Jones RAF
Cpl. A. Thorell RAF
Cpl. V.C. Belding RAF
Cpl. Pepper RAF

*Source: Pemberton, L., (Daughter of
Wing Commander R. G. Kellett), 303
Squadron booklet produced to
accompany a Memorial Service held
for Wing Commander Ronald
Gustave Kellett 30th August 2014.*

SWIĘTO DYONU – R.A.F. EXETER.
10.9.1941.

GRUPA OFICERÓW.

1. Por. Prędecki.	13. Por. Neyder.	25. Por. Szkop.
2. Kpt. Gołoński.	14. F.O. McDonald /Bryt/.	26. Por. Maliński.
3. F/L. Male /Bryt/.	15. Kpt. Sawczyński.	27. Por. Murzyński.
4. Ks.K. Kończewski.	16. Ppor. Podgórski.	28. Por. Reutt.
5. Ks.K. Starostka.	17. Por. Mika.	29. Por. Lazarowicz.
6. Kpt. Antonowicz.	18. Ppor. Puzyna.	30. Por. Bukowiecki.
7. Por. Alexandrowicz.	19. Por. Szablowski.	31. Por. Gayzler.
8. Por. Lewandowski.	20. Por. Zaremba.	32. Por. Pfleger.
9. Por. Zwoliński.	21. P.O. Kownacki.	33. Ppor.Hrynaszkiewicz.
10. Por. Gierasimowicz.	22. Por. Andrzejewski.	34. Por. Swierz.
11. Por. Karwowski.	23. Ppor. Maxymowicz.	
12. F.O. Holt,P.G. /Bryt/.	24. Por. Damsz.	

GRUPA PERSONELU LATAJĄCEGO.

1. F.O. Maliński.	18. F.O. Bukowiecki.	37. Sgt. Illaszewicz.
2. F.O. Andrzejewski.	20. Sgt. Armanowski.	38. Sgt. Niewolski.
3. Sgt. Zakrocki.	21. F.O. Szablowski.	39. Sgt. Sadowski.
4. Sgt. Lewandowski.	22. P.O. Puzyna.	40. Sgt. Domański.
5. Sgt. Pietrzyk.	23. P.O. Maxymowicz.	41. Sgt. Jarzembowski.
6. Sgt. Rudel.	24. F.O. Szkop.	42. Sgt. Kaliszewski.
7. Sgt. Leskowski.	25. F.O. Swierz.	43. Sgt. Woźny.
8. Sgt. Bałucki.	26. F.O. Damsz.	44. Sgt. Kubas.
9. Sgt. Pelik.	27. Sgt. Turzański.	45. Sgt. Ostrowski.
10. F.O. Neyder.	28. Sgt. Wisthal.	46. Sgt. Erndt.
11. P.O. Pfleger.	29. Sgt. Szempliński.	47. F/L. Sawczyński.
12. Sgt. Modro.	30. Sgt. Trawicki.	48. F.O. Zwoliński.
13. Sgt. Jarzembowski.	31. Sgt. Putz.	49. F/L. Alexandrowicz.
14. Sgt. Zaniewski.	32. Sgt. Murzyn.	50. W/G. Antonowicz.
15. Sgt. Jankowiak.	33. Sgt. Snieżkowski.	51. F/L. Lewandowski.
16. P.O. Podgórski.	34. Sgt. Lissowski.	52. P.O. Gayzler.
17. F.O. Lazarowicz.	35. Sgt. Karais.	53. F.O. Karwowski.
19. F.O. Mika.	36. F.O. Prędecki.	

Above image: Group of officers 307 Squadron.
Right: Group of flying personnel 307 Squadron.

ESKADRA "A".

1. AC. Piekut.
2. AC. Król.
3. Sgt. Skóra.
4. AC. Antonowicz.
5. Sgt. Podgajny.
6. AC. Windys.
7. AC. Lorentowicz.
8. Sgt. Bałucki.
9. AC. Dej.
10. AC. Hetmański.
11. AC. Siuda.
12. AC. Rembalski.
13. F.O. Szablowski.
14. P.O. Podgórski.
15. F/L. Sawczyński.
16. F.O. Bukowiecki.
17. F.O. Zwoliński.
18. F/L. Alexandrowicz.
19. F/S. Skierczyński.
20. F.O. Andrzejewski.
21. F.O. Lazarowicz.
22. F.O. Swierz.
23. P.O. Maxymowicz.
24. Cpl. Czeręda.
25. Sgt. Jarzembowski.
26. F.O. Maliński.
27. Sgt. Pieczeniewski.
28. Cpl. Wesołowski.
29. Cpl. Urbaniak.
30. Sgt. Wasilewski.
31. AC. Krupowicz.
32. AC. Orzepowski.
33. AC. Kruszewski.
34. F/S. Wójcik St.
35. Sgt. Pelik.
36. Sgt. Sadowski.
37. Sgt. Armanowski.
38. Sgt. Kaliszewski.
39. AC. Struk.
40. Sgt. Erndt.
41. Sgt. Lissowski.
42. Sgt. Domanski.
43. AC. Rudawski.
44. AC. Geldarski.
45. AC. Fouer.
46. AC. Cieciński.
47. AC. Grzyb.
48. AC. Sąsiadek, Wł.
49. AC. Gawinkowski.
50. AC. Kubaczka.
51. Cpl. Zalewski.
52. AC. Palak.
53. AC. Leszczuk.
54. Cpl. Kacalski.
55. AC. Rottermund.
56. Sgt. Zajakała.
57. AC. Brzezicki.
58. AC. Szatkowski.
59. AC. Stępniewski.
60. AC. Pawłowski.
61. AC. Berent.
62. AC. Mietelski.
63. AC. Pisch.
64. AC. Piwowar.
65. AC. Grodz.
66. Cpl. Buziak.
67. Cpl. Kalwa.
68. AC. Dzendzera.
69. AC. Sniegowski.
70. AC. Olasek.

Above: Squadron A 307.

SWIĘTO DYONU - R.A.F. EXETER.

10.9.1941.

ESKADRA "B"

1.	AC.	Zaparciński.
2.	AC.	Kaszubowski.
3.	AC.	Gajko.
4.	Cpl.	Bałasz.
5.	AC.	Kopikowski.
6.	Sgt.	Rudel.
7.	AC.	Ketryniak.
8.	AC.	Janusiewicz.
9.	AC.	Frydriger.
10.	AC.	Sąsiadek, M.
11.	AC.	Zelazko.
12.	AC.	Wybiera.
13.	Sgt.	Karais.
14.	Sgt.	Putz.
15.	F.O.	Neyder.
16.	P.O.	Puzyna.
17.	P.O.	Gayzler.
18.	F/L.	Lewandowski.
19.	F/S.	Jakimowicz.
20.	P.O.	Pfleger.
21.	F.O.	Szkop.
22.	F.O.	Karwowski.
23.	Sgt.	Wisthal.
24.	Cpl.	Witkowski.
25.	Cpl.	Kmieciak.
26.	Sgt.	Trawicki.
27.	AC.	Urbaś.
28.	AC.	Kalisz.
29.	Sgt.	Pietrzyk.
30.	Sgt.	Woźny.
31.	Sgt.	Niewolski.
32.	Sgt.	Illaszewicz.
33.	Cpl.	Ignarski.
34.	Sgt.	Lewandowski.
35.	Sgt.	Sanok.
36.	Sgt.	Zaniewski.
37.	Sgt.	Kubas.
38.	Sgt.	Zakrocki.
39.	Sgt.	Szempliński.
40.	AC.	Gorzelańczyk.
41.	Sgt.	Turzański.
42.	Sgt.	Ostrowski.
43.	Sgt.	Jankowiak.
44.	Sgt.	Piłat.
45.	AC.	Czternastek.
46.	AC.	Szramka.
47.	Sgt.	Murzyn.
48.	Sgt.	Stawidło.
49.	Cpl.	Złotek.
50.	AC.	Cieślewicz.
51.	AC.	Korbecki.
52.	AC.	Osięglewski.
53.	AC.	Zielonko.
54.	AC.	Lasoń.
55.	AC.	Wesoły.
56.	AC.	Karp.
57.	AC.	Szymoniuk.
58.	AC.	Ziomek.
59.	AC.	Kubica.
60.	AC.	Seremak.
61.	AC.	Babijczuk.
62.	AC.	Jarosiński.
63.	AC.	Adamczyk.
64.	AC.	Sitko.
65.	AC.	Szymczak.
66.	AC.	Gajewski.
67.	AC.	Pikulski.
68.	Sgt.	Laskowski.
69.	AC.	Przybylski.
70.	AC.	Czarnecki.
71.	AC.	Pater.
72.	AC.	Siatecki.

Above: Squadron B 307.

SWIĘTO DYONU - R.A.F. EXETER
10.9.1941.

ESKADRA "M" TECHNICZNA.

1.	AC.	Wichrowski.
2.	AC.	Michalski.
3.	AC.	Frankland /Bryt/.
4.	Cpl.	Gajda.
5.	AC.	Wróblewski.
6.	AC.	Konarzewski.
7.	AC.	Siennicki.
8.	AC.	Szafran.
9.	AC.	Nawrot.
10.	AC.	Cesarz.
11.	AC.	Malinowski.
12.	AC.	Jabłoński.
13.	AC.	Sakwiński.
14.	AC.	Tymruk.
15.	AC.	Okołów.
16.	Sgt.	Kokalski.
17.	AC.	Cummnis /Bryt/.
18.	F/S.	Troczyński.
19.	F/S.	Harwaziński.
20.	F/S.	Staszyszyn.
21.	F/S.	Gutowski.
22.	F.O.	Murzyński.
23.	F.O.	Gierasimowicz.
24.	F.O.	Kownacki.
25.	F/S.	Drost.
26.	Sgt.	Schuchard.
27.	Sgt.	Krzewiński.
28.	AC.	Bachadur /Bryt/.
29.	AC.	Wilson /Bryt/.
30.	AC.	Herheson /Bryt/.
31.	AC.	Zieliński.
32.	AC.	Chwieralski.
33.	Cpl.	Polakowski.
34.	AC.	Skornia.
35.	AC.	Żyrawski.
36.	Cpl.	Szkudlarski.
37.	AC.	Kus.
38.	AC.	Kulik.
39.	Cpl.	Sobański.
40.	Sgt.	Jagiełło.

41.	Sgt.	Tomaszewski.
42.	AC.	Messerschmidt.
43.	Cpl.	Kapuściński.
44.	Cpl.	Cholawo.
45.	AC.	Stefaniak.
46.	AC.	Ratajczak.
47.	Cpl.	Ostrowski.
48.	AC.	Kaniuka.
49.	AC.	Wijaszko.
50.	AC.	Pietrasik.
51.	AC.	Reyne /Bryt/.
52.	AC.	Redfren /Bryt/.
53.	AC.	Woroncow.
54.	AC.	Rakowski.
55.	AC.	Nowakowski.
56.	AC.	Panasiuk.
57.	AC.	Jończyk.
58.	AC.	Kaczor.
59.	AC.	Winnik.
60.	AC.	Sanicki.
61.	Sgt.	Wodławik.
62.	AC.	Setkowicz.
63.	AC.	Bielawski.
64.	AC.	Gawarski.
65.	AC.	Walaszek.
66.	AC.	Filipiak.
67.	AC.	Drąg.
68.	AC.	Chrzanowski.
69.	AC.	Niedzielski.
70.	AC.	Stachów.
71.	AC.	Kulisa.
72.	AC.	Czmejduch.
73.	AC.	Moździerz.
74.	AC.	Byrczek.
75.	AC.	Mochliński.
76.	Cpl.	Gryc.
77.	AC.	Trzebuniak.
78.	AC.	Piwoński.
79.	AC.	Majkut.

Above: Technicians 307 Squadron.

Chapter 7
The Night Owls

While Londoners sought refuge in underground stations or make-shift Anderson shelters during the blitz, the populations of Bristol, Plymouth and Exeter took to trekking out to the countryside each evening to escape the raids. Bristolians traipsed up to the Mendip hills or other outlying rural areas, and Devonians headed for Exmoor and Dartmoor. Throughout the blitz and beyond members of the Polish 307 Squadron were among the pilots protecting British cities and coastline in the South West. Designated night fighters they were quickly nick-named the Eagle Owls and earned a well-deserved reputation for being fearless in combat. Established on 10th September 1940 they were initially hampered by being equipped with Defiant aircraft rather than front gun fighters, and their first posting to the rain soaked, windswept Isle of Man did nothing to lift their spirits. Their Adjutant, Flight Lieutenant C.A. Hale recorded:

There were very poor station facilities at Jurby, and work was unin-teresting. We did convoy patrols during the day with no sign of the Hun! We then moved to Squires Gate but had a ten-day delay because of snow. At Squires Gate we had our first combat and life became much more interesting with much night flying. In March 1941 we moved to West Colerne and here we had the full facilities of a Fighter Command Station. We were only a month at Colerne, but it was a happy month. In April 1941 we came to Exeter and Squadron Leader Antonowicz assumed command.[1]

By this stage West country cities had already taken a severe battering at the hands of the Luftwaffe and some incoming raids occurred with little or no warning. On 17th March 1941, for example, eight bombs were dropped on a playing field in Devonport, killing a number of boys who had been leisurely playing football only a few moments earlier. A few days later, on the 20th, the

Right: Franciszek Kornicki with 315 Squadron playing chequers at RAF Northolt, waiting to be scrambled into action. Their names chalked on blackboard to their left.

Above: Polish night fighter.

city's hospital was among the many buildings that were bombed in a night raid that lasted nearly four hours. Four nurses and nineteen children were killed. Virtually all of Plymouth had been bombed and by the early hours of 21st March the whole city was on fire. The bombing continued the following night and enemy planes managed to destroy St Andrews Church and all of the municipal buildings, including the Guildhall.[2]

It was no wonder therefore, given the devastation of Plymouth and surrounding cities, that when 307 Squadron arrived at RAF Clyst Honiton in Exeter they were welcomed with open arms by a grateful public. Given the responsibility for guarding South West England and specifically for intercepting night raids the pilots had undertaken rigorous training in night flying techniques. Kazimierz Budzik recalled:

Sometimes you would fly at night with moonlight, but very often there was no moonlight. This chappie was making photos of Exeter. A few days later there was a raid on Exeter. I was in standby, then intercepted a Messer 109. I'd seen him at 1,000 yards and opened fire. I was with another one (member of Squadron). The plane started losing power, I lost that plane and it went. In anger I pulled my mask and as I did that, I lost consciousness. When I woke, I was about 9,000 feet diving towards the sea when I pulled plane out. The Messer was too high, and already over 30,000 feet. But everything new was excitement and I survived being shot down twice! German pilots in early stages of the war were fairly aggressive but later stages they were trying to avoid contact. We also used to take part in air sea rescue.[3]

Above: Stanisław Skalski receiving medal.

Navigation at night was far more difficult than during daylight hours, but new developments in radar systems such as airborne interception (A.I.) and ground-controlled interception (G.C.I.) did much to improve this situation. However, Defiant aircraft were not totally reliable and mechanical problems caused numerous accidents. These included Sgt. J. Mikszo and Sgt. S. Kondras who were both injured on 2nd December 1940 in their Defiant L7035, P/O. S. Szablowski and Sgt. Broda injured on 23rd December 1940 in Defiant N1641 and Sgt. K. Bocheński and Sgt. Frąckiewicz who were killed in their Defiant N3314 on 17th February 1941.[4]

In August 1941 the unit was re-equipped with Beaufighters and conversion training flights took place on most days. Squadron members were hopeful that this conversion would improve tactical fighting and reduce the number of accidents. Extracts from their official operations record book give some idea of training sessions and operations:

3.8.41. Weather conditions improved slightly, and cross-country flights were made during the day. H.Q. No. 10 Group letter 10G/S.9168/Org/47 dated 1st August 1941 was received advising that the unit is to be shortly

R.A.F. Form 540

See instructions for use of this form in K.R. and A.C.I., para 2349, and War Manual, Pt. II., chapter XX., and notes in R.A.F. Pocket Book.

21793 Wt. 32805/2533 400,000 12/39—M.C.& Cr-51-5658

OPERATIONS RECORD BOOK

of (Unit or Formation) No. 307 Polish Squadron, R.A.F.

Page No. 102

No. of pages used for day

75

Place	Date	Time	Summary of Events	References to Appendices
Exeter.	1.8.41.		Weather conditions generally were unfavourable and day flying was restricted. No night flying was possible owing to bad weather. **Total flying hours :-** 6.05 (day) NIL (night)	
	2.8.41		Weather conditions were again poor. A day searchlight co-operation exercise was carried out and further searchlight co-operation flights were made at night. **Total flying hours :-** 7.50 (day) 1.15 (night)	
	3.8.41		Weather conditions improved slightly and cross country flights and Army cooperation flights were made during the day. H.Q. No. 10 Group letter 10G/S.9168/Org/47 dated 1st August 1941 was received advising that the Unit is to be shortly re-equipped with Beaufighters Mark I. Conversion of all squadron pilots to Beaufighters is to be carried out at Exeter, using the experience and instructional qualifications in the squadron. Training of A.I. operators is also to be carried out at Exeter under the direction of P.O. Kornacki who will be posted to the Unit for that purpose. Great satisfaction, on the part of the whole Squadron, is felt regarding the re-equipment with Beaufighter aircraft. Weather conditions were favourable for night flying and searchlight co-operation flights were carried out. **Total flying hours :-** 8.20 (day) 2.25 (night)	
	4.8.41		Weather conditions were poor and day flying was restricted. A.G.C.T. test flight was carried out during the morning. Two British LAC, Observers (Radio) posted from No. 3 Radio School reported for duty. Weather deteriorated during the evening and night flying was not possible. **Total flying hours :-** 6.20 (day) NIL (night).	
	5.8.41.		Very strong winds made the air to ground firing arranged for Warmwell impracticable and this had to be cancelled. Day flying was restricted and night flying was confined to searchlight co-operation flights. **Total flying hours :-** 6.50 (day) 1.10 (night).	

Above: Summary of events August 1941.

re-equipped with Beaufighters Mark I. Conversion of all squadron pilots to Beaufighters is to be carried out at Exeter, using the experience and instructional qualifications in the squadron. Training of A.I. operators is also to be carried out at Exeter under the direction of P.O. Kownacki who will be posted to the unit for that purpose. Great satisfaction on the part of the whole squadron is felt regarding the re-equipment with Beaufighter aircraft. Weather conditions were favourable for night flying and searchlight co-operation flights were carried out.

Total flying hours: 8.20 (day) and 2.25 (night)

4.8.41. Weather conditions very poor and day flying was restricted. A.G.C.T. test flight was carried out during the morning. Two British LAC. Observer (Radio) posted from No. 3 Radio School reported for duty. Weather deteriorated during the evening and night flying was not possible.

Total flying hours: 6.20 (day) NIL (night)

5.8.41. Very strong winds made air to ground firing arranged for Warmwell impracticable and this had to be cancelled. Day flying was restricted, and night flying was confined to searchlight co-operation flights..

Total flying hours: 6.50 (day) 1.10 (night)

8.8.41 Weather conditions were again unfavourable, and flying was restricted. H.Q. Fighter Command signals Q. 162 and Q163 dated 7th August were received advising that the squadron is to be re-equipped with Beaufighter II aircraft and not Beaufighter I as previously advised. Weather conditions were suitable for night flying and searchlight co-operation flights were carried out.

Total flying hours: 5.40 (day) 2.00 (night)

14.8.41 Weather conditions improved, and day training continued. Training on Blenheim aircraft was continued. G.C.I. practice flights and co-operation exercises were carried out with Defiant aircraft. Beaufighter II aircraft R.2443, R.2446, R.2447 and R.2449 were delivered by No. 19 M.U. under authority 41G/1113. Weather conditions were unsuitable for night flying. P/O. Kownacki reported for duty from High Ercall today.

Total flying hours: 14.15 (day) NIL (night)

20.8.41 Day training continued under favourable weather conditions on Oxford and Beaufighter aircraft. G.C.I. practice flights and cross countries were carried out with Defiant aircraft. Beaufighter aircraft R. 2315 was delivered by No. 13 M.U. under authority 41G/11378. Oxford V.3975 was collected and flown to No. 409 squadron under authority Headquarters Fighter Command signal: Q.805 dated 19th August 1941. Weather conditions were suitable for night flying and searchlight co-operation exercises were carried out, together with night flying practices. Blenheim aircraft L.8438 was slightly damaged in a taxying accident, Pilot, P/O. Neyder, when the aircraft ran off the runway onto soft ground. Damage is reparable at the unit.

Total flying hours: 18.00 (day) 4.40 (night)

24.8.41 Weather conditions were good and flying training on Beaufighter aircraft continued. Defiant N.3490, pilot Sgt. Turzański, B, was damaged when after touching down the aircraft turned violently to the left and despite the pilot's efforts to straighten up by means of the brake, by the end of the run the undercarriage collapsed.

Total flying hours: 15.50 (day) NIL (night)

30.8.41 Weather conditions were suitable and day training on Beaufighter, and Blenheim aircraft continued throughout the day. P/O. Świerz reported for duty as Observer (Radio) u/t from No. 30 M.U. Sealand. Beaufighter II aircraft R2315 crashed when port engine failed immediately after take-off. Sgts. Malinowski and Modro were both injured, and the aircraft completely wrecked. Fire broke out on the ground and the aircraft was burnt.

Total flying hours: 14.40 (day) NIL (night)

To the dismay of the Squadron, although Beaufighters were fitted with two Merlin engines, they were also initially susceptible to mechanical failure. Indeed, pilots began to refer to them as 'flying caskets.' A series of accidents followed, culminating in the tragic death of their highly popular Squadron Leader Antonowicz, who was killed on 23rd October along with his observer Flying Officer Karwowski, when trying to land his Beaufighter with a defective engine. This was a bitter blow which seriously affected morale.

Once all technical issues were resolved however, Beaufighters did go on to prove their worth. Flight Lieutenant Hale explained:

November 1941 gave us our big success with the Beaufighters, and Squadron score started to mount up. Enthusiasm was at fever heat and the depression caused by the death of Squadron Leader Antonowicz

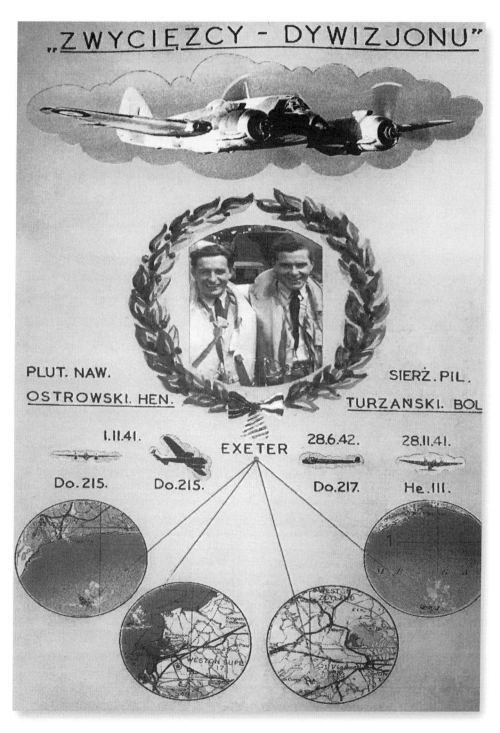

Above: Artwork by members of the 307 Squadron.

Above: Artwork by members of the 307 Squadron,
including drawings to remember fallen comrades.

was overcome. This activity was followed by a long period when the Hun would not come near Exeter and combat was non-existent. Wing Commander Brejnak took over at a difficult period, a bad period when there had been a lot of fatal accidents.[5]

The sterling efforts of Polish pilots were very much appreciated by west country communities and they were inundated with correspondence. Many letters contained invitations to social gatherings, words of encouragement and hand-made cards, along with tokens of affection or talismans. Writing on 24th November 1941 nine Plymouth women expressed their gratitude:

Dear Sir,

Please convey our grateful thanks to the 'night fighter' who shot down the 'Fritz' plane on Sunday night. The thrill repaid us for some of the agonies endured in the blitz on Plymouth. We wish he could have heard the cheers of the people in the city streets; it would have done his heart good. May he have the best of good luck in the future and happy landings. We shall be proud if you could acknowledge this letter in the Evening Herald or Western Morning News.

Signed: nine Plymouth women.

P.S. Hope the enclosed mascot will 'shoe' the 'Jerries' away.[6]

With their dashing good looks, innate charm, courtesy and exuberance for life, the Polish airmen became a firm favourite with the young and old alike. Across the length and breadth of the country, romances between youthful British ladies and Polish menfolk blossomed amid the bleakness of black-outs and bombs. The Poles also endeared themselves to the men of their localities, playing football matches against Home Guard teams, joining them for off-duty drinks, playing snooker, cards and darts. They organized concerts, dances and even cocktail parties to raise funds for those who had been bombed out of their houses. Furthermore, because the 307 Squadron remained in Exeter for a considerable time, they became fully integrated with their neighbours.

While members of RAF Squadrons were busy shooting down Luftwaffe planes on the Home Front, the British eighth Army began an offensive in Libya. Then on 7th December, Japanese forces launched a brazen attack on Pearl Harbour that virtually destroyed America's Pacific fleet. The following day Britain and America declared war on Japan, and on 10th and 11th December America declared war on Germany and Italy. Furthermore, after some intense political

Polish Airmen host a party for bombed out children in Oxford.

wrangling, Churchill managed to convince President Roosevelt that the Allies needed to concentrate their efforts on winning the war in Europe before tackling the war in the Far East. Consequently, as Christmas 1941 approached a tangible spirit of optimism accompanied the Home Front celebrations.

The Poles energetically organized and supervised children's Christmas parties, and in quiet times they carefully made unique cards to send to loved ones near and far, not knowing if they would ever reach their destinations. They also drew poignant pictures of pilots who had been killed, either in action, or by accident. Some of these hand-crafted cards depicted their fallen comrades as stars in the night sky, while drawings often showed a pilot kneeling by a gravestone marked with a cross bearing the fallen pilot's name.

As the Squadron ushered in a New Year there was a period of reflection, stagnation and at times despondency. Morale was eventually lifted by the onset of the Luftwaffe Baedeker raids in the spring of 1942, as F/Lt. C.A. Hale reported:

Enemy activity and concentrated raids on Exeter and Bath provided the antidote in early May and the Squadron score again rose steadily. We were re-equipped with Beaufighter VI aircraft. Of the personnel officers, NCO's and airmen I have nothing but praise. To Poland and the Poles, I have an apology for not discovering their sterling qualities before this war. I believe, my months with this Squadron have given me an understanding of the Poles, and when this war is over and Poland is restored to its rightful place in Europe I shall consider it my very pleasant duty to visit Poland and complete my Polish education.[7]

Named after a nineteenth century German tourist guidebook, Baedeker raids focussed on British cities renowned for their historic buildings and cultural significance. They were also known by the Luftwaffe to be less well defended than other major cities. Bath, Exeter, Canterbury, Norwich and York were among those targeted. The worst night for Exeter was that of 3rd/4th May when ninety enemy aircraft bombarded the city centre with high explosives, parachute mines and incendiaries. Against this fierce attack four night-fighter aircraft of the 307 Squadron took off to intercept the raiders and succeeded in shooting down four enemy bombers before they could drop their deadly cargo. One hundred and sixty-three Devonians died that night and enemy attacks persisted throughout the summer months. The Daily Sketch reported on 6th August:

Nazis lose a Fifth of Night Raiders
By destroying six of thirty German raiders sent over early yesterday morning, Britain's defence against the night bombers scored one of their biggest successes.

A Polish Night Fighter Squadron, which already had the distinction of destroying four raiders in a night got three. One Beaufighter pilot and his observer shot down two of them within a few minutes of each other off the South West coast.[8]

When weather conditions deteriorated in the autumn however, raids lessened in number and frequency. As September approached, Wing Commander Jan Michałowski wrote to local and national dignitaries to invite them to the Squadron's birthday party on 10th September. The Minister of Economic Warfare, Hugh Dalton was among those to write an acceptance letter, stating:

The British Airmen and the whole British nation are very proud of our comradeship with the Polish Airmen. We are fighting side by side in

order that your beautiful and historic country shall again be happy
and free, and the menace of German barbarism finally eliminated
from Europe.
With Cordial Greetings to the officers and men of your Squadron.
I am Yours Most Sincerely
Hugh Dalton[9]

Other demonstrations of comradeship between Britain and Poland followed, and on November 15th Wing Commander Jan Michałowski presented Exeter's mayor with the Polish national flag as a token of the mutual affection and respect which existed between members of the Squadron and the local people.[10] The Squadron's fan base continued to expand, conspicuous in a further deluge of letters. Personal experiences of the blitz had also generated a greater empathy with the Poles as revealed in the following poem written by a lady named Betty:

Salutation

Tall of shoulder lean of build.
Keen blue eyes when on the kill
Ripping pilot smashing Ace
Always laughing in deaths face
Can he always be like this?
Laughing, joking in the mess
Silence as he wakes one morning
Just another vacant place
Who can tell what he is thinking?
As he talks and laughs with us
Who knows of the hidden anguish?
He may have within his head
Tears of anger for the memory
Of a now disbanded race
Dragged through mud and toil and torture
By a hard-exacting race
Can we wonder at his hardness?
As he mouths that hated name 'HUN'
Yes, we know what he is going through
Young, impulsive, clear and kind.
Dear to me, as to the skies
Never far from our winds

> *We who now have known sadness*
> *Sunk to depths of misery*
> *Understand the more his heartache*
> *And the longing to be free*
> *We salute you and the boys of the 307*
> *For all that you have done for Britain and your own beloved land[11]*

Mrs K. Goddard, of the Women's Voluntary Services was among those who thanked the Poles for their contribution in defence of Exeter:

> *I hope some-day we may all be able to show our deep gratitude to you by helping you all when you get back to your homes in Poland.[12]*

Signs that the war had turned in the Allies favour were numerous by the autumn, and government ministers began to contemplate post-war reconstruction. On 1st December 1942 the Beveridge Report was published, which became the blueprint for the welfare state. In cities and towns across the country, people queued in streets for hours on end to buy a copy of the report, and thousands of copies were airlifted to members of the British armed

***Above:** Photographs taken by members of 307 Squadron.*

forces serving abroad. In compiling his report, Liberal economist Sir William Beveridge had encompassed the mood of the people—all of whom supported the notion of a better, fairer and more egalitarian post war society. Designed to provide care from the cradle to the grave Beveridge recommended the introduction of a national health service, family allowances and social security payments. The impact of Beveridge was enormous. His report encouraged an idealistic focus—a sense that everyone was fighting together to establish a brighter future. As such, it did much to shore up British morale.

The nature of conflict was changing however, and it became increasingly clear that 307 Squadron would soon be required to undertake offensive roles rather than remain on the defensive. There were also occasions when they were used as a diversionary force to entice enemy aircraft away from allied bomber raids aiming for targets across occupied Europe. The Squadron was then re-equipped with Mosquito aircraft, which were considerably faster than Beaufighters. But on 21st March 1943, when Jan Michałowski tried to land his Mosquito on one engine in high winds, he and his co-pilot Stanisław Szkop struggled to control the landing; both tragically died. Two days later hundreds of local people turned out to pay their respects at the funeral. Michałowski's death occurred just weeks before the Squadron was posted to Swansea. This was followed by a further move to Cornwall, with rest periods at East Lothian.

These changes in assignments were prompted by significant allied advances being made elsewhere. The earlier loss of Singapore in February 1942 had been a bitter blow to the British government, but in October the same year Field Marshal Montgomery and the Eighth Army attacked German forces at El Alamein for the second time. Massive numbers of British and American troops were sent to reinforce the area. Their combined material superiority was unquestionable. With Rommel's defence weakened by his failing health the Germans were unable to do anything other than to make a final stand. Losses were heavy on both sides, but eventually the Germans retreated along the coast. 'Operation Torch,' which began on the 8th November, sealed Rommel's fate. Anglo-American forces landed in Algeria and Morocco and Rommel was caught between the Western Desert Force, which was advancing from Egypt, and the Anglo-American Force, which was in pursuit from Algeria. On 23rd January1943 the allies regained Tripoli. In a fit of pique German forces in occupied Poland burned down seven villages as a punishment for Polish participation in this campaign. For a while Rommel was able to fall back, and

Above: Photographs taken by members of 307 Squadron.

even take command of a campaign in Tunisia. However, Anglo-American troops greatly outnumbered the remnants of Rommel's Panzer divisions, and by 4th February Libya had been totally taken over by Anglo-American forces. Following these decisive allied victories in North Africa, the war in the desert was virtually over by the middle of May and 240,000 German and Italian soldiers were captured. In the meantime, Russian forces had mounted a strong and lengthy counteroffensive at Stalingrad inflicting a costly defeat on German forces. Coupled with the successful Allied invasion of Sicily, the Italian government realized that the tide of war had turned against them and surrendered to the Allies in September; and on 13th October declared war on Germany.

Henceforth, 307 Squadron were primarily deployed on offensive operations, covering large sections of the Atlantic Ocean, and the Bay of Biscay. Other Polish Squadrons were often assigned roles as bomber escorts for American Flying Fortresses and divers (to bomb VI &V2 rocket stations). They also took part in 'Rodeo,' 'Rhubarb' and 'Circus' operations, and played a crucial role in the gathering of intelligence information.

Chapter 8

Circuses, Rhubarbs, Rodeos and Ramrods

During the Battle of Britain, the exploits of Bomber and Coastal Commands were completely overshadowed by the spectacular dog fights of Fighter Command. But while the latter were busy engaging the enemy overhead, Bomber and Coastal Command were ensuring that German barges earmarked for Operation Sealion were destroyed before they could even embark.

Sergeant Władysław Łapot flew the first Fairey Battle mission against German barges and was disappointed not to receive the recognition he deserved:

> *I do not understand why crews of both our Squadrons are not considered for the Battle of Britain clasp. We flew against the German invasion fleet, that was a real threat for the Britons, and our actions directly prevented their attack. No less than actions of the fighter pilots. Without doubt German soldiers were there for a reason, waiting for the signal.[1]*

Coastal Command defended British shipping operating in the Mediterranean, the Middle East and Africa. Closer to home they vigilantly patrolled the English Channel, Bay of Biscay and the Atlantic Ocean, safeguarding shipping lanes and defending supply lines. They also launched offensive bombing missions, destroying German ships situated near occupied Europe. During the first few years of the war British shipping losses were catastrophic. German U-boats lurked in the Atlantic, waiting to sink merchant ships laden with food stuffs, hoping to starve the British people. Józef Jaworzyn, flying with 304 Squadron explained:

> *Something had to be done to stop these incredible losses, at times it was disastrous. Coastal Command required two pilots and flights were about ten hours duration. Bay of Biscay was our main area. It was very active in terms of U-boats going across the Channel. They were going through from French bases and German aircraft protected them. One time we attacked—firing at fighters as we approached. Then, at twenty-five feet, just at the point when I was about to drop bombs there*

Above: Shatterproof plexiglass windows designed for noses of A-20 attack bombers, pictured at Long Beach California plant of Douglas Aircraft Factory.

was a white flare. I dropped the bombs but saw nothing. I managed to get away then both engines stopped. Sometimes this was because of the nature of petrol used; efficiency of petrol. It would foul up the spark plugs. I had this happen, I can recall that.[2]

While flying with 306 Squadron Kazimierz Budzik patrolled the coast:

Up North it was boring, but even then, you had to be on guard. You had to watch your own shipping. You had to keep some distance, or you could be hit by your own.[3]

121

During the summer of 1941 RAF bombers targeted Rouen and Lille with limited success. In addition to guarding coastal waters Polish pilots along with their RAF counterparts acted as escorts for bombing raids. Reports of these raids were classified. The following combat report for example, compiled by Flight Sergeant Brzeski posted to 317 Squadron was designated secret and addressed to Sector Intelligence Officer at RAF Pembrey:

I took off at 15.55 as No. 2. Blue section, B Flight. We were detailed to escort convoy. At 16.20, F/Lt Szczęsny warned me of aircraft flying low in direction of convoy. Then we were 600 yards away, aircraft was identified as Ju 88, which jettisoned bombs in sea 300 yards before convoy. Blue one attacked from astern and I gave boost and came round to port beam of enemy aircraft, opening fire at 250 yards and closing into 50 yards astern. I saw firing from rear gunner. When I had no more ammunition, I turned right and flew 1.1/2 minutes at same height as Ju 88. Ju 88 lost speed from 220-120 and the tail touched the water twice and then the wing, after 40 seconds more, the enemy aircraft hit the water, sinking immediately. A few yellow objects remained on the surface and after 1 minute I identified one enemy airman. In my cockpit I saw white smoke and I thought it came from my guns though temperature of Glycol was 100 C. I landed at 16.40. After landing I found one bullet in my radiator. I had fired all my ammunition.[4]

Above: *U.S. aircraft production.*

In November the same year Sgt Brzeski reported:

I took off at 11.05 hours in 317 (P) Squadron. We were detailed to form Escort Cover in a bomber sweep to Lille. On the way home, 5 miles east of St Omer, at 17,000 feet I saw one Me109 attacking one of the Spitfires of the Close Escort at 14,000 feet below and in front of me. I dived to attack the Me109 and fired a first long burst from above, left, astern, opening at 250 yards closing into 100 yards. The Me109 burst into flames, dived very steeply and fell, burning well and leaving a trail of thick black smoke. I followed him to 6,000 feet when I suddenly noticed a Focke Wolf 190 approaching with its square wing tips and tail, and its radial engine. He turned sharply right and dived apparently out of control, swinging from side to side, and I lost sight of him at 2,000 feet. A moment later I saw a Focke Wolf 190 coming straight at me from ahead. It opened fire and one bullet hit but did not penetrate my bullet proof windscreen. I dived down after him firing one short burst. At 1,000 feet I set course for home.

Me109 seen by two other 317 pilots to hit the ground.

Claim*: One Me 109F destroyed, one Focke Wolf 190 damaged.*[5]

For a while, the new German Focke Wolf 190 posed a challenge for the RAF. It flew fast and low to avoid radar detection and was initially used for air defence over the continent, and later to mount raids on coastal towns. It was also deployed in other fighter roles such as attacking bomber escorts. By this stage

Above*: Polish flag of 317 Squadron 1940 stating that love will sacrifice.*

Above: Mascot of bomber squadron pictured on gun of aircraft.

Hurricanes were confined to ground attacks and short-range bombing missions and the Spitfire Mk V was outclassed by the FW 190. Therefore, the Spitfire Mk IX with its supercharged Merlin 61 engine, was duly brought into operation to combat the Focke Wolf 190. Subsequently, Air Chief Marshall Sir Arthur Travers Harris, nicknamed Bomber Harris was appointed head of Bomber Command with a remit to take the War to Europe. Or in the words of many Londoners—to give Jerry a taste of his own medicine! In a speech to a hard-pressed British nation Bomber Harris asserted:

> *The Nazis entered this war under the rather childish delusion that they were going to bomb everyone else and nobody was going to bomb them.*

At Rotterdam, London, Warsaw and a hundred other places they have
put their rather naïve theory into operation. They have sowed the wind
and now they are going to reap the whirlwind.[6]

Aided by the introduction of the Avro Lancaster and Halifax bombers RAF
Squadrons mounted large scale night bombing raids on German cities in the
spring of 1942. Daylight raids were also launched on targets in occupied France
and Belgium, but losses were considerable. Two hundred and eighty fighter
aircraft (mainly Spitfires) were shot down between January and the end of May.
In response, Fighter Command Headquarters issued an order to limit
operations to coastal targets.[7] It was also clear that some pilots found bombing
raids too hot to handle. As Bob Nawarski recalled:

We lost quite a number of pilots. One pilot—he just couldn't take it. The
same chap almost bumped into me on the wing. This chap would
release his bombs too high. He said he was trying to cover us, but there
was no aircraft in that area. His nerves couldn't stand it and he was
taken off operations. In the First World War he probably would have
been shot. We didn't ostracise him, but we didn't want to fly with him
again. A few months afterwards I went to his wedding. He changed his
name to an English name.[8]

RAF 'Circus' missions (small daylight bombing raids accompanied by fighter
escorts designed to encourage enemy aircraft to engage in combat) were
stepped up and included Rhubarbs, Rodeos and Ramrods. 'Rhubarb' attacks
comprised of small groups of aircraft, which were frequently flown in inclement
weather to destroy ground targets in occupied France and Belgium. Losses
were high however, partly because of aggressive anti-aircraft fire. As Kazimierz
Budzik recalled:

The worst thing for a fighter was flying air to ground, because you knew
you'd be shot at. They don't aim at you they made a barrage and we
had to go through it. There was no other way. Never had time to think
and when you actually do a thing there is no fear. Then you've got rid
of fear.[9]

Larger numbers of fighter aircraft took part in 'Rodeos,' these acted as bait to
encourage enemy aircraft to engage in dog fights. They usually flew over enemy
territory in reasonable weather at high altitudes. Ramrods meanwhile consisted
of heavily escorted bombing raids. Yet despite these new tactics RAF losses
continued to rise. On 19th August Fighter Command committed five PAF

Above: Eleanor Roosevelt visiting a Women's Auxiliary Air Force camp.

Squadrons along with fifty-five RAF Squadrons to provide air cover for a combined operations attack on Dieppe in preparation for an Allied invasion of Europe. Fighting was fierce above the Normandy fishing port, and one hundred RAF aircraft were destroyed with the loss of fifty-two pilots. Many of these were captured.

RAF Squadrons were also involved with intelligence operations. Churchill had established the Special Operations Executive (SOE) giving them orders to 'Set Europe Ablaze.' Agents were required to disrupt Nazi war aims by any means possible and galvanise the native populations of occupied territories into taking action against their enemies. Although the SOE was not without its detractors. Naturally the British wanted to secure an ultimate Allied victory over the Nazis, but there was considerable opposition to the methods proposed by the SOE. Some ministers thought it was simply 'not quite British' to get involved in things such as sabotage and undercover work on such a grand scale. They claimed there was something quite distasteful about the whole process. Yet it was clear to military Chiefs of Staff, who were contemplating an invasion of Europe, that the populations of occupied Europe needed to be prepared for such an invasion. Given their earlier reluctance to fight, they certainly needed to gauge the level of French loyalty to the Vichy government. As one of the SOE lectures on operational propaganda stated:

> *Today it is useless for our propaganda merely to persuade Frenchmen that the Boche is a swine. It must also instruct Frenchmen how to kick the Boche out of France. Our propaganda to enemy and occupied countries is now mainly operational; and, as such, should always contain joint elements of persuasion and action.*[10]

A Polish section of SOE was trained at Audley End in Essex but underground Resistance movements could only operate effectively if they were adequately supplied with guns, explosives and other sabotage equipment. It was relatively straightforward to deliver supplies by parachute to members of the French resistance, even when dates and times were changed at the last minute.

Enlisting the co-operation of the BBC World Service, a system was developed whereby pre-arranged coded messages were slipped into personal message bulletins, which were broadcast between 7.30pm and 9.30pm. Through these bulletins BBC presenters were able to inform SOE agents when a parachute drop was imminent. Romantic and innocent sounding messages thus became the signal for hundreds of Resistance groups across Europe to leap into action.

Supplying Poland with sabotage equipment however, posed significant dilemmas and prompted intense political wrangling. Moreover, Allied objectives gave priority to the French while Polish considerations took a back seat in strategic policy formation. Therefore, although Polish agents were experts in intelligence operations, having supplied Britain with much of the information required to decipher the Enigma code; a shortage of available aircraft seriously hampered the delivery of supplies. [11]

In the meantime, unaware of these political disputes, Polish pilots continued with their missions. Flight Sergeant Brzeski reported on Ramrod 26:

Whilst flying at 25,000 feet, ten miles S.W. of Dunkirk, my section of four aircraft, to the left, had difficulty in keeping up with the Wing Commander's right-hand turn and Sgt Malinowski and I lost contact with the formation. We climbed and turned and then saw Squadron 8 miles away already leaving the French coast. I then noticed 800 yards away and at 20,000 feet 1 F.W.190 which I could only catch slowly as I

Above: *Ploughing fields in preparation for the construction of temporary airfields.*

was obliged to 'weave' for safety. At 600 yards a Spitfire dived at the F.W. breaking off right, while the F.W. swerved left giving me advantage to catch up. I gave 2 short bursts from 350-250 yards and he dived, swerving. I followed firing 3 more bursts and he ceased evasive action steepening his dive. I continued my dive to 2,000 feet and then pulled out and I saw my F.W. crashing into the sea about 400 yards away.
Rounds fired: 2 cannon 45 rounds
4 m/g   400 rounds [12]

Three months later Brzeski described his participation in a Rodeo attack five miles off Calais:

At the moment when my Squadron approached Gravelines my Flight Commander gave the order to turn right because on the starboard side we saw a combat, and I saw a parachute and a F.W. 190 and Spitfire circling and manoeuvring. I was in the starboard four and I saw 1 F.W. 190 turning left at about 7/8,000 feet. I attacked the E/A and gave a long burst from 350-300 yards. The F.W. 190 dived towards France. I followed this F.W. and fired a second burst astern from 300-250 yards. I noticed flashes on the port side of the E/A's fuselage and clouds of black smoke began to pour out. The F.W. 190 went straight down to the sea, completely out of control. As I was going to give a third burst, I noticed on my port side the tracer bullets of an E/A passing me. I made a sharp left turn and last saw my own F.W. 190 diving at the same angle 2 miles from the coast, 150 feet up and about to hit the water. I claim this F.W. 190 destroyed. Meanwhile the second F.W. 190 turned right and up and I re-joined my Squadron. Camera gun carried and exposed.
Rounds fired: 58 each of 2 cannons
Each m/g 303…140 rounds [13]

In addition to bombarding occupied Europe and obtaining vital intelligence by means of reconnaissance, experienced airmen were also required to achieve air supremacy over North Africa and the Mediterranean. At the beginning of 1943 fifteen highly skilled Polish pilots volunteered to join an elite team of fighters flying under the leadership of Squadron Leader Stanisław Skalski (Wing Commander from December 1943). Flying the new Spitfire Mk IX's over North Africa they quickly became known as Skalski's Circus and were attached to 145 Squadron. A few months later German forces capitulated in Tunisia, by which time pilots in Skalski's Circus had shot down thirty enemy aircraft. In July

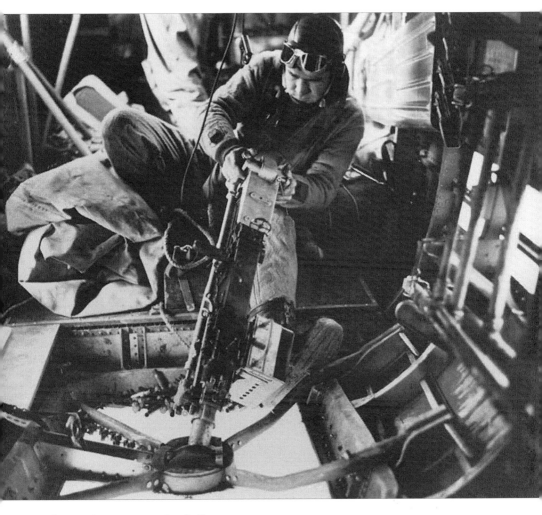

Above: Gunner manning belly gun.

Skalski assumed command of 601 Squadron (County of London) providing much needed Allied air support over Malta, Sicily and Italy. With an Allied victory secured in North Africa, Malta was no longer under siege or at risk from invasion. Churchill therefore describing Sicily and Italy as the soft under belly of Europe, proceeded to move Allied forces up through the Mediterranean. Strategically this policy was designed to remove Italy from the war, coax Turkey into supporting Allied combat missions in the Balkans and provide a base from which to mount ground force attacks into Austria and Germany. Moreover, by engaging the enemy in Italy, to some extent the Allies succeeded in restricting the number of German troops available to fight the Russian front.

The Italian campaign, and growing demands for aircraft in the Far East, drained RAF resources on the domestic front. Despite this situation Ramrod operations continued apace. Marked as secret, the Wing Intelligence Combat Report, Ramrod S.36, dated 6th September 1943 details the activities of Northolt Polish Wing 303 and 316 Squadrons, and four aircraft of 124 Squadron. The report also demonstrates how well pilots worked together to shoot down enemy aircraft:

General

24 Spitfires IX, 12 each of 303 and 316 Polish Squadrons, and 4 Spitfires VII from 124 Squadron, left Northolt at 17.02 to act as top cover to 72 Marauders attacking Amiens Marshalling Yards.

Rendezvous was made with whole formation over Dungeness. When about 20 miles West of Amiens, Operations warned Wing about two groups of E/A South East of Amiens, and one formation of E/A over target Amiens.

S/Ldr. Żurakowski, leading Wing, ordered Wing to increase speed, and Wing drew ahead of beehive and after circling target at 26/29,000 feet., saw about 12 Me. 109's at 25,000 feet flying from West down sun towards the main formation.

316 Squadron

Seeing the E/A approaching the main formation, 316 Squadron went to attack. Only four pilots closed range to open fire, but not seeing the results, did not claim. After pulling up from attack, most pilots saw 2 aircraft in flames South of Amiens.

303 Squadron

Squadron, making right hand turn East of Amiens, saw about 8 Me. 109's flying behind our main formation and 6-8 F.W. 190's in pairs approaching the target area from South West, all E/A flying about 25,000 feet. 303 Squadron immediately dived down and attacked E/A and the story of their combats is below:

S/LDR Falkowski J.

I dived to attack with my Squadron from about 28/29,000 feet. When approached to first pair of F.W. 190 to about 500 yards I gave two long bursts, closing range to 300 yards. After second burst E/A started smoking with black smoke. In that time, I noticed flashes of tracer passing near my cockpit and when I pulled up another F.W. 190 passed

immediately my Spitfire. After I turned to the left and saw about 5,000 feet below my F.W. 190 in flames, and about one mile to the South another F.W. 190 also with smoke and flames, destroyed by F/Lt. Wandzilak. The combat took place about 10 miles South of Amiens at 20,000 to 16,000 feet between 1755 and 1800 hrs. Camera exposed.
Ammunition *2 Cannon 60 rounds each*
4 m/g   80 rounds each.

F/Lt *Wandzilak S.*

I was leading the starboard section of 303 Squadron when making right hand turn East of Amiens and seeing about 8 Me 109 and some F.W. 190's behind main formation, I dived to attack. Closing the range behind one of the F.W. 190's I opened fire from about 500 yards closing to 200 yards. I gave one long burst and to avoid collision with E/A I pulled up my Spitfire. When again I dived behind F.W. 190 I noticed black smoke coming from E/A and flames. In this same moment I have

Above: *American Airmen with bomber aircraft.*

seen one Spitfire spinning without tail. There was no smoke or flames coming from Spitfire. Witnesses of my claim are S/Ldr. Falkowski and P/O Śliwiński. The combat took place about 10 to 15 miles South of Amiens at 25,000 to 16,000 feet between 17.55 and 1800 hrs. Camera exposed.

Ammunition *2 Cannon 25 rounds each*

4m/g   150 rounds each

Most pilots of 316 Squadron saw two aircraft in flames South of Amiens which confirm the above-mentioned claims.

P/O Śliwiński W.

I was number two of F/Lt. Wandzilak's section. When we dived to attack, I noticed a group of 7-8 Me. 109's and second group of 5-6 F.W. 190's. I attacked nearest Me 109 giving one short burst. I broke off the attack because I was attacked by another Me 109 with a yellow nose. I saw also F/Lt Wandzilak attacking a F.W.190 which went down smoking. I went to attack again and opened fire at one of the 5 F.W.190's flying from South West. I gave one long burst from 400 yards astern. I noticed the flashes on wings and fuselage of F.W. 190. E/A rolled up, pulled up on the back, and went down in flames. The combat took place South West of Amiens at 24,000 feet between 1800 and 1805 hrs. Camera exposed.

Ammunition *2 Cannon 25 rounds each*

4 m/g   75 rounds each

F/ Sgt. Chudek A.

I dived to attack on formation of 5 F.W. 190, approaching from South West. I followed behind two F.W.190 from 27,000 feet to about 6,000 feet in a South Easterly direction but seeing E/A below I pulled up and climbed into sun keeping to the left of Amiens. When I was about 15 miles W.N.W. of Amiens at 16,000 feet I noticed one F.W.190 flying to the North. I kept good position to attack, and when 200 yards behind E/A I gave one long burst, closing range to 50 yards. F.W. 190 immediately caught fire and went down vertically. Witness of my claim is F/Lt Sobolewski of 316 Squadron, who saw my F.W. 190 in flames. Attack took place at 1806 hrs. Camera exposed.

Ammunition *2 Cannon 30 rounds each*

4 m/g   50 rounds each

HALIFAX LL126 flight on 21st November 1944 at 19.30

THEY SACRIFICED THEIR LIVES TO SAVE OTHERS

Fg Off J. KISIELEWICZ
Plt Off J.T. MAŁKOWSKI
Flt Sgt W. RUCIŃSKI
Sgt .S. RADOŃSKI
Sgt. F. KRUSZCZAK
Sgt. S. JAQUSZCAK
Sgt. S. JURKA

Rest in Peace

g Ashton, 2'

Above: Memorial to the seven Polish Airmen who died when their Halifax bomber crashed in a field in Long Ashton near Bristol.

Sgt. Czeowski
I was flying in section led by F/Lt. Wandzilak. When over Amiens area I heard order 'Go to attack.' I dived with my section and saw about 10 E/A (Me 109G's and FW 190's). I selected one pair of Me 109G (recognised by gun blister under each wing) and approached behind them. When about 400 yards away I gave one three seconds burst to the leader of this section, seeing flashes of my bullets on the cockpit of Me 109G. The E/A pulled up and went down with grey smoke and later in flames.

> *S/Ldr Żurakowski, Wing leader of this operation, saw my Me 109 in flames diving down. Camera exposed.*
> **Ammunition** *2 Cannon 18 rounds each*
>   *4 m/g   40 rounds each*
>
> *After these combats Wing returned to base (aircraft in groups and singly) and landed at 1910 hrs.*[14]

Photographs were taken when bombers activated their bombs, to make sure that targets were hit. Bob Nawarski was surprised to find one of his bombing successes on the silver screen:

> *We were in Le Havre area and saw an empty boat and I attacked. I knew I had probably hit it. Then during a second attack the whole thing exploded and showed on my picture. A few weeks afterwards I saw the same picture in the cinema on Movie-tone news. I said to my friend: 'That's the bloody thing I hit!'*[15]

Following the Dam-buster successes earlier in the year Bomber Harris mounted a costly series of attacks on Berlin in November. By March 1944 over seven thousand RAF crew members were killed and one thousand six hundred and eighty-two aircraft destroyed.[16] Bomber Command, which had been severely criticised at the time, and subsequently, for launching area bombing raids in addition to purely military offensives, shifted focus towards specific targets near Normandy beaches ear-marked for invasion points. Raids were also conducted over Calais and other potential landing areas to divert enemy attention away from Normandy beaches. Crucially, RAF bombers brought down communication lines, disrupted transport links and destroyed basic infrastructure in preparation for Operation Overlord. Meanwhile, the United States Army Air Force, which had already mounted daylight bombing sorties over Northern France and further afield across Germany, significantly increased bombing operations. These largely rendered the expensive RAF Circus operations superfluous to requirements.

Chapter 9
D-Day and beyond

In the first few months of 1944 newspapers were full of stories relating to vigorous Allied advances. Preparations for a second front, code-named Operation Overlord, prompted a myriad of training exercises for Allied forces, a large-scale re-organization of RAF Squadrons and the formation of a Second Tactical Air Force (2TAF). In readiness for an invasion of Normandy Allied aircraft were moved closer to planned invasion sites, and numerous RAF Squadrons were relocated to East Sussex and Kent. Polish Squadrons 302, 308 and 317 now formed 131 Fighter Wing of 2TAF. Accommodated in tents adjacent to purpose built advanced landing grounds they prepared the way for the invasion of occupied Europe and provided vital air cover for the D-Day landings.

In the build-up to Operation Overlord Bob Nawarski was involved in fighter sweeps, dive bombing and escorting American and British bombers to marshalling yards in Normandy. On D-Day he rose before dawn:

I was woken up at 3am on the 6th June and we assembled in the briefing room. They told us the invasion was starting. We were told to patrol Neptune beach Normandy. We took off at 4 am. The sight was incredible, an Armada of ships in different shapes and sizes. You felt you could almost walk across them they were so tightly packed. No enemy aircraft on the way. Also, we had surprise, and total cover in the air. We spent two or two and a half hours patrolling, come back to refuel, and then back again. Beaches being bombed by ships was quite a sight. Three or four miles from shore the air would actually shake! In the afternoon we flew again, half of the Channel to France then a ribbon of ships going back to get more troops. We lived in tents. We were the first Squadron to land in France itself, North East of Bayeux. They had prepared a landing strip for us; long enough to land and take off. Then we could refuel again and patrol the beaches. You felt so elated that exactly four years after I left this country I was returning—this time as a liberator. But the first French man I met was a farmer who asked: 'who is going to compensate me for the land being used as an airstrip?' You felt like shooting him! It was such a climb down from the elation.[1]

Kazimierz Budzik was another pilot operational on D-Day:

We went over before barges hit the coast. It was frightening to see the Navy when barges hit coast. We had a fantastic view as they were chopping into coast. We were the first fighter planes over there. After a few days we landed in France a few times. We attacked more or less air to ground dive bombing. We just destroyed them, ripped them to pieces. Animals after invasion were all dead. We saw Germans with their hands up. We still had anger so showed little mercy. They were already beaten.[2]

Flight Lieutenant Werner Kirchner flew with 2TAF assigned to cover American forces landing on Utah beach at 6.30 am:

After take-off at 04.30 we reached the Channel where below us an armada of 4,000 ships was heading towards Normandy. The entire French coast from Le Havre to Brest was an inferno. We saw the 87th and 101st Airborne American divisions landing behind the German line as well as the assaults on the beaches. Few people know that the Germans were unable to take an aerial picture of the invasion for two weeks. Every time we saw a German aircraft approaching the region, we would pounce on it from all directions...Allied domination of the air at that critical time was practically complete.[3]

Most German casualties were under the age of nineteen, but older, hardened SS officers were also captured. All appeared to be under the impression that England was already occupied by Germans. A nurse working in Normandy wrote to her matron from the frontline:

The very first patient on D-Day was a German Officer—I can't remember his rank—an army officer with shrapnel in his buttocks, and he demanded to be taken to German occupied England. On being told that no part of England was occupied—it took a lot to convince him of this—he became frantic with fright because he had been told that English doctors operated on prisoners of war without anaesthetic. It took five of us to hold him down to give him an anaesthetic. Some of the soldiers were most peculiar, especially the SS officers. They didn't want to survive. Some of them pulled out their intravenous tubes when

Above: *An armed guard protects an American Flying Fortress aircraft.*

Right: *Artwork by members of 307 Squadron depicting their offensive role against enemy held territory in Europe 1943-1945.*

> *they were having a blood transfusion. They just wanted to die for the Fuhrer, and they jolly well did! They used to walk around and blow their tops. They were very arrogant. When we were busy nursing, we had bed, stretcher, bed, stretcher in the reception room; the place had been a little school and we had stretchers galore. You could hardly put your feet between them. We were luckily wearing our battledress kit because the Germans used to mess on the floor, and we had to put our gaiters on so that we didn't get the bottom of our trousers filthy. They were all in a very queer state.*[4]

Some members of Allied forces were captured by the Germans, including pilot Lech Stanisław Łaszkiewicz, who encountered enemy aircraft on the second day of the invasion:

> *He went straight down into the deck. I continued my turn. Just as I got to the coastline my engine seized and the propeller just stopped in mid-air. I had a choice of going over high-tension wires or underneath them. I thought if I went over the top, I couldn't have got back on the ground at a reasonable angle without breaking the aircraft, so I went under them. There were other wires and large telegraph poles. I didn't want to bale-out because it was the second day of the invasion and anything dangling on a parachute would be a target. I didn't fancy that, so I put nose down and eventually hit the ground and slid around. In the meantime, I kept all guns firing, mainly to keep the Germans away but also because six guns firing had quite a decelerating effect, a braking effect. Anyway, I went to the ground. Anti-invasion poles chopped the wings more or less like matchsticks. Unfortunately, I put my head down and when aircraft eventually came to a stop after a mighty row of banging and shattering noise, the whole fuselage was bound in barbed wire. It tore my battledress, but it didn't touch me. I stopped with most of the wings missing—just sort of stubs. I was on top of a German slit trench. First of all, it was very quiet after all the noise. Then I heard a little bird tweeting about and I thought Oh I'm still alive*

and I'd better get out quick; but unfortunately the Germans just popped up from the trench on both sides pointing their guns at me and said: 'Oh zee war is over for you come!' [5]

Finding himself back in France again, and in enemy hands Łech instinctively remembered his training. He knew not to divulge any information under any circumstances, and realised very quickly that his captors knew nothing about the invasion:

It was amusing in a way because they got me down and underneath the slit trench there was a big bunker underground with doors and windows facing into the trench. They got me inside and started laughing and joking at me. I had a Mae West on me which had pictures on it. One of the Squadron members was a bit of an artist. In Mae Wests we had lights like cigars with a screw cap. One picked it up and said what's this? He started unscrewing the cap and I thought I'll let him, but then I had second thoughts. I thought if that thing goes off in his face and blinds him, I'm not going to be very popular. I couldn't explain this, so I grabbed this thing and he said nein nein nein and grabbed it back. He got stroppy with me saying yaya and nein nein. I shouted at him: 'It is fire!' He twigged then what it was, and that was my first experience of being a prisoner of war.

We had Polish flashes on our arm, and they must have known because they said Poland on them. I think they were regular army characters they weren't S.S. or anything. Eventually I was marched away to a headquarters in a chateaux and taken to a room in a loft. Sometime later there were steps and they brought an American pilot in. He had American uniform and wings on him. I looked at him and he looked at me. I thought I have heard about this sort of thing; they are going to put us together to ask questions, so I wasn't going to talk to him. Likewise, he wasn't talking to me either, so we just sat there looking at each other. Eventually we started talking to each other and he said: 'What's your name?' I said 'Łaszkiewicz' and he said: 'Mine is Mazurek, so we laughed a bit. It transpired he was also a Mustang pilot. He got shot down over the coast.

Interrogations continued over the course of several days. During the journeys to prisoner of war camps the captured allies were escorted by old German soldiers:

As we drove near railway yards, we saw that Holland was flattened. Germans were laughing saying: 'Look what you've done to your Allies.' Very soon after we went into a tunnel which eventually emerged in Germany. One of the Americans said: 'Aha, look what we've done to you.' That didn't go down very well..

We were in an interrogation camp in Bavaria for ten days. I was taken to the officer's mess had a shave and they gave me food and drink. They started talking about Poland in general. But we had been warned not to say where we were from in Poland, because the system was to grab your family and you had to talk or else! I knew by then that the Russians had moved in quite a way into Poland and had the Eastern part back again. I let slip that I came from way behind Russian lines and they lost interest in me after that.[7]

Łaszkiewicz spent the remainder of the war in a camp near the Baltic region.

Allied forces meanwhile fought to establish strategic bases in Normandy. As an integral part of 2TAF, 131 Wing had provided vital air cover for the D-Day landings. Henceforth, from a base at Plumetot, they flew reconnaissance and bombing missions, efficiently gathering intelligence while systematically wreaking havoc on enemy troops and communication systems. Additionally, they were operational during the Battle of Falaise Pocket:

At the end of the Battle the bottleneck was held by General Maczek's Polish 1st Armoured Division who were assaulted by desperate German forces from within and without the pocket. They held their ground for three days of desperate hand to hand and close quarters fighting until virtually all their ammunition was expended. Nonetheless, they blocked the last escape route effectively and over 60,000 German troops were killed or taken prisoner by the Allies and 2,000 tanks and assault guns were lost by the enemy.[8]

As Polish pilots continued to mount intelligence and offensive missions alongside their RAF comrades, back in their beleaguered homeland the men and women of Warsaw were rebelling against their German oppressors. A mass rising began on 1st August:

The people of Warsaw were ready to fling themselves into this last thrust to rid themselves of the German occupation. On the same day on the Western Front the 1st Polish armoured division became involved in

Right: *Troops preparing for D-Day landings.*

> *France on the Falaise sector. They fought there for the next few weeks*
> *with the plight of Warsaw constantly in their thoughts.*[9]

The Polish Home Army had initiated a surprise assault on German troops in Warsaw in the belief that Soviet forces across the river Vistula would quickly supply them with more weapons and soldiers to assist them in their struggle. Instead, the Red Army did nothing. Despite several requests from Churchill and Roosevelt imploring Stalin to intervene, the latter, still nursing a hatred for Poland because of an earlier Polish victory over the Red Army, which had culminated in the Peace of Riga in 1921, simply stood by and watched the devastation unfold on his doorstep. Stalin even refused permission for Allied aircraft to land and refuel; therefore, the only available aerodrome bases from which to deliver vital supplies to Warsaw, were in Brindisi, Bari and Foggia in Southern Italy. The Polish 1586 Squadron and other members of the PAF, flew alongside RAF Squadrons and the United States American Air Force (USAAF). Primarily using Halifax and Liberator aircraft they made long and treacherous supply missions over enemy territory to Warsaw. Losses were significant, forty-one Allied aircraft were shot down and two hundred and sixty Allied Airmen killed. Flying in a Consolidator Liberator with 178 Squadron, Sergeant Lyne recalled his flight over Warsaw on the night of 13th/14th August 1944:

Above: *Squadron Leader Eugeniusz Horbaczewski with his Mustang.*

Above: Kazimierz Budjik in front of his Spitfire at Ghent airfield Belgium.

The whole wing looked to be on fire and the most amazing thing was that at this particular time the anti-aircraft shells were coming through the bottom of the aircraft and going out through the top. I likened them then, and still do, to cricket balls on fire. They looked about the size of a cricket ball and they were glowing. The 20mm stuff I would have thought. I could virtually have put my hand out and caught them.[10]

The Warsaw uprising ultimately failed, as yet again the Polish people were left to fight their oppressors with little allied assistance:

On 10th September:

The Germans began a final clearing up operation. Systematically all civilians, men, women and children, were rounded up and shot. Hospitals were burned with doctors, nurses and patients still inside. All remaining buildings were levelled, so that no settlement could ever exist there again.[11]

Two days later, Stalin belatedly allowed some American aircraft to land on Soviet airstrips after they had dropped food and supplies over Warsaw. But this meagre

of (Unit or Formation) ....No. 300 (POLISH) Squadron.

No. of pages used for this ...14

	Summary of Events	SECRET.	References to Appendices
	OPERATIONAL FLYING HOURS - DAY - 183 Hours 50 Minutes.		
	OPERATIONAL FLYING HOURS - NIGHT - 598 Hours 45 Minutes.		
	NON-OPERATIONAL FLYING HOURS - DAY - 180 Hours 30 Minutes.		
	NON-OPERATIONAL FLYING HOURS - NIGHT - 99 Hours 05 Minutes.		

GRAND TOTAL. —— 1,062 Hours 10 Minutes.

Bomb Tonnage for the month of July 1944 amounted to 754 Tons - Made up of the following:-
18 x 4,000 lb. H.C. - 20 x 2,000 lb. H.C. - 50 x 1,000 lb. M.C. - 573 x 1,000 lb. G.P. U.S.A.
297 x 1,000 lb. S.A.P/U.S.A. - 507 x 5000 lb. M.C. - 196 x 500 lb. G.P/L.D. - 50 x 500 lb. G.P.
522 x 500 lb. G.P./U.S.A. - 240 x 500 lb. Clusters U.S.A. 'J' Type.
Ammunition:- 70,000 rounds .303 - Operational. - 13,500 lb. .303 - Practice.

The following article appeared in the Press having been released by the Air Ministry News Service.
The Air Gunner referred to is 782874 Flight Sergeant P. ZENTAR and the other two members of the crew
who helped this airman are 704108 Flight Sergeant Derewienko J - Mid Upper Gunner and 781951 Sergeant
Bialucha J.
The article begins:- A POLISH rear - gunner blown out of the turret of his Lancaster over Caen by
blast from an anti- aircraft shell, was flown back to England hanging from the bomber by only one
foot. The Lancaster was one of the force of more than 1,000 bombers which attacked targets near
Caen early on July 18. Telling the story of the rear gunner's remarkable escape, the Polish Mid-
Upper Gunner said - "Three seconds before we bombed a shell burst just to the right of the rear
gunner. The blast swung his turret beyond its usual position, ripped open the door at his back,
and sucked him out of his seat. He fell backwards, finishing up head downwards, but with his left
foot somewhat jammed. That was the only thing that saved him. I broke a hole in the vision panel
and pressed a valve which moves the turret, so as to turn it back and jam his leg firmly. I was afraid
of breaking his leg, but something had to be done. Then I leaned over and held his shoes, but they
began to slip off. I clawed at his trousers, but they began to tear. As we flew on over France I
hung on to him somehow however and kept on holding the valve at the same time. The Germans were still
firing at us and the Pilot had to throw the aircraft about. When we got over the channel I shouted
for help and the Flight Engineer got a rope which we dropped out from the turret. The Engineer supported
the rear gunner and gave him one end of the rope. I had to grip the engineer with my free hand while
still pressing the valve, as I was afraid he would fall out too. But the rear gunner managed to tie
the rope round himself and then we fastened it firmly to the inside of the aircraft. We found an
airfield soon after we crossed the English coast, got permission to land and signalled that we had
a wounded rear gunner. We landed very well indeed; it was wonderful. As the Lancaster touched down
the rear gunner managed to swing to one side and keep his head out of the way of the ground. When we
stopped he was bleeding from the ears and mouth, but he was not badly hurt, though he was suffering
from severe shock." (NOTE - This aircraft landed at Tangmere with a full bomb load, the bombing
equipment being put out of action by flak).

T. POZYCZKA.
Wing Commander, Commanding, No. 300 (POLISH) SQUADRON.

Report detailing the extraordinary story of a gunner from 300
Squadron flown back to England from France hanging from a
Lancaster bomber by one foot.

assistance was too little too late. Pockets of Polish resistance continued to fight on until early October but then all efforts subsided. Clearly, Stalin had purposely and callously enabled the Nazis to destroy the Polish Home Army in order to further his own territorial ambitions.

Meanwhile, on the Home Front a mere seven days after the D-Day invasion, the first German V-1 rocket hit London. These pilotless monoplanes were quickly nicknamed Doodlebugs or flying bombs and signalled the beginning of a period known as the 'mini blitz'. Loaded with a one-ton warhead the V-1 travelled at three hundred and fifty miles an hour to a pre-set target. Since there was little warning of their arrival there was no time for anyone to seek shelter before they exploded. Such attacks, usually carried out in broad daylight, were viewed as sinister and alarming. Dr Arthur Walker of St Thomas's hospital recalled:

> *It was an anxious time because you heard them coming, then they went quiet, then they exploded. One day a block of flats was hit just north of Hammersmith—there were appalling injuries.* [12]

In total nine thousand, five hundred and twenty-one V-1 rockets were launched against London and Southern England. RAF fighters and anti-aircraft fire destroyed four thousand, six hundred and twenty-one of these.

Above: Part of 178th enemy aircraft shot down by 303 Squadron 3rd July 1942.

Right: Polish baby receives his late father's DFC medal. His father was Polish fighter pilot ace Marian Belc.

Training flights for bomber crews were stepped up and in one tragic incident, Polish aircrew demonstrated extreme bravery when their Halifax V number LL126 aircraft crashed at Long Ashton near Bristol. As soon as the crew began to experience severe engine problems the pilot deliberately steered the plane away from the village community into a nearby field. All seven men on board were killed. David Neal witnessed the crash:

> *I remember standing by a wall and looking over. I was only ten at the time. I looked across the field and what was the remains of the plane were totally engulfed in flames. People did try to rescue the men, but the plane was evidently on fire before it crashed, and they really couldn't get near it to do an effective rescue.*[13]

On Christ the King Day 21st November 1944 an Act of Remembrance was incorporated into the service at All Saints Church Long Ashton, in honour of the seven Polish men who died. The service began with a recorder group playing traditional Polish dances and the Polish Folk Song Suite. Led by the Crucifer a procession of local people laid wreaths near a Memorial Plaque naming the Polish air crew:

> *Pilot—F/O. Jerzy, Szymon, Kisielewicz P.1989 PAF aged 33*
> *Fl/Eng: Fl/Sgt. Witold Wacław Ruciński 792655 PAF aged 33*
> *Nav:P/O. Jan Tadeusz Małkowski P. 2852 PAF aged 26*
> *W/Op/AIR/Gnr: Sgt. Franciszek Kruszczak PAF 705020 aged 32*
> *Air/Bmr: Sgt. Jan Sylweriusz Radoński PAF 704017 aged 27*
> *Air/Gnr: Sgt. Stanisław Jurka PAF 706472 aged 30*
> *Air/ Gnr: Sgt. Stanisław Jaguszczak PAF 706780*

The Polish National Anthem was played, and the service pamphlet translation into English affirmed Polish hopes of a liberated Poland:

Poland has not yet succumbed,
As long as we remain,
What the foe by force has seized, sword in hand we'll gain.
March March Dabrowski!

March from Italy to Poland!
Under your Command
We shall reach our land.[14]

With this poignantly expressed hope for the future freedom of their precious homeland in sight, Poles continued to assist their Allies by every means possible.

Above: *General Sikorski decorates Polish Airmen.*

Hot on the heels of the V-1 came the V-2 supersonic strategic missile. Components of the new V-2 rocket were smuggled into Britain courtesy of the Polish Home Army and intelligence services prior to its launch. A thorough examination of these components revealed that although V-2 rockets were much faster than the V-1, and therefore much harder to destroy in the air, they often experienced severe technical problems. Furthermore, due to the speed of impact damage was frequently inflicted underground. Nevertheless, the five thousand V-2s fired specifically at London still caused considerable structural damage and hundreds of casualties. The best way to protect the Home Front from these latest incursions was to prevent the rockets from being launched in the first instance. As the National press reported:

> *Specially picked and briefed Spitfire pilots yesterday planted all their bombs in a Dutch railway station and siding used to park V-2 supply trains. Typhoon bombers, based in Belgium bombed railway wagons in marshalling yards believed to be laden with V-2S on their way to the Hague.*[15]

Tadeusz Jerzy Krzystek of the Polish 131 Wing recalled:

> *We were spreading a steel netting in defence of London chasing Doodlebugs. Home defence was based near Ashford. We had to change boost to open up at three hundred feet if necessary. Many killed at that time. I was more afraid of the Doodlebug's pumping noise than I was of the Doodlebug itself.*[16]

V-1 and V-2 launching sites were heavily camouflaged, but intelligence information was reasonably accurate in supplying location details to Allied forces. Bolesław Drobiński took part in patrolling operations::

> *At this time Spitfires were taking off every twenty minutes, we had additional petrol. We would fly one hundred and ten miles across the Channel to Hague area where V-2s were launched. We would go there early in the morning and patrol the area so V-2s could not be launched. Germans didn't want to disclose launching pads.*[17]

Kazimierz Budzik also led attacks on V-2 sites and survived being shot down twice:

> *I was above a raider when I was shot down. I was leading. After attack I pulled to the right to start firing. I turned around and smoke was coming from my engine, so I crash landed. The 49th Division picked*

Above: Kazimierz Budzik's wrecked Spitfire with a member of armed Dutch militia.

me up. Some Dutch people said the Germans had gone. Thank God for it! I go up with the Intelligence people. Two days later I was leading a dive-bombing expedition. They try to anticipate you and you tried to anticipate them. Then I was hit, and oil started coming out all over me. I knew I could steer to British side. The Spitfire was so safe and great. A Desert Rats Lieutenant came to me with a pistol and said: 'Are you alright?' I told him who I was and said: 'Put that away.' Then they invited me to the mess for dinner. I was very lucky—very few people survived being shot down twice.[18]

In a bid to free France from occupation over 265,000 Germans were killed or wounded and 350,000 were captured as prisoners of war.[19] Yet despite the allied advance, the Germans were reluctant to surrender even though they were under attack from both sides. The Russians in the East were marching towards Germany's heartland, and the American, British and French armies had advanced as far as the frontiers of the Reich. Simultaneously, Allied air raids on Germany were imposing and debilitating. Short of manpower, and with diminishing levels of industrial production, Germany was in the process

Right: *Stanislaw receiving*
congratulations for his medal.

of being reduced to rubble. Eager
to regain control of his Western
flank, Hitler propelled his military
machine towards Antwerp, hoping
to split American and British
forces. Thus, on 16th December
Germany launched a major
counteroffensive, which became
known as the Battle of the Bulge
because of the bulge it created in the American lines. Initially, American forces
sustained heavy losses and fell back, but against the odds they held fast and
the Germans were unable to break through. Eisenhower instructed Patton to
attack the German left flank, and promptly placed American units cut off by
communications disruptions under the command of Montgomery. A
coordinated response was maintained, and the Battle of the Bulge became the
largest land battle fought by the Americans during the entire Second World
War. A combination of swift and substantial Allied reinforcements and isolated
bouts of heroism successfully halted the German advance. Difficult terrain,
bad weather and fuel shortages had impeded German progress, but once
weather conditions improved in late December the Allies were able to bring
fighter planes to bear on the situation.

Bob Nawarski took part in the Allied advance into Holland:

> *Once Allies had broken into main German defences the advance was
> quite swift. We were attacking fleeing trucks. When main break-out
> came it was like a roller coaster towards Belgium aerodrome. Ghent
> was supposed to be a city of a thousand churches—there were certainly
> churches on every ruddy street. Main activity was near Holland
> border—Antwerp. We were bombing trains. We lived in individual tents
> and you had to dig your own bed; it had to be three feet lower than the
> ground to protect you from artillery fire. Mess tent and food was okay.
> From the air we could see columns of troops, transport and tanks. It
> was pandemonium, and with all the anti-aircraft fire it wasn't a piece
> of cake. Sites were littered with bodies—a terrible sight. It was a bit
> different from fighting Germans in the air, because you knew then it*

Above: *General Sikorski pictured with Wing Commander Gordon Sinclair and members of the Polish Air Force and Royal Air Force.*

was either you or him. There you felt like you were murdering them. I wouldn't like to have been a German in these days. Later I was based in Germany, near Hamburg. We had German waiters in the officer's mess. My best friend Szczerbiński was a very good pianist actually and played in the officer's mess. Virtually on the last operational flight he was hit by anti-aircraft fire. The sad part was that it was nearly the last operational flight of the war. Another day and he would have been alright.[20]

151

Nawarski's best friend F/Lt. Leslaw (Leszek) Szczerbiński was the last member of the PAF to be killed in action during the Second World War, when his Spitfire was hit by anti-aircraft fire on 4th May 1945. He was a gifted pianist and composer who had earlier composed the official 308 Squadron Song.[21] This tragic loss of life occurred a mere three days before Germany's unconditional surrender.

The Germans were already in retreat by January 1945. Subsequent battles in the Rhineland in February and March inflicted major defeats on Germany, and remaining German units were clearly in disarray and marred with a sense of defeatism. By April an Allied victory in Europe was assured, and on 30th April Hitler committed suicide, blaming all and sundry for the German defeat. On 2nd May, German forces in Italy surrendered and by 8th May the German High Command had capitulated. The actual signing of the surrender took place at 2 a.m. on 7th May, and by midnight on the same day people across Britain were celebrating like never before. Public holidays were granted for 8th and 9th May and street parties were in full swing up and down the country. Church bells joyfully rang out across the land, and Britain's naval vessels sounded a siren of salute in honour of the long-awaited victory. In a cathartic, and symbolic bombing raid on 25th April 1945, Polish airmen of 300 Squadron joined the Allied bombers who destroyed Hitler's mountain retreat in the Bavarian Alps. But victory in Europe for the Poles still far from home, was a bitter-sweet moment. Tadeusz Jerzy Krzystek described his feelings:

The V E bells were ringing. It was a joyful day. But the moment I learned the war had ended, it was like I had to stop doing something, and I felt emptiness. I cried and I couldn't stop myself. I knew there was still a struggle to free Poland.[22]

Polish airmen and armed forces, who had fought with such incredible valour throughout the war, were confronted with the stark realization that while most of Europe had been liberated; their own country remained in the iron grip of the Russian dictator who had invaded their homeland six years earlier.

Left: Flt. Lt., Leslaw (Leszek) Szczerbiński killed by anti-aircraft fire on 4th May 1945.

Chapter 10
The legacy

Although the fate of Poland was sealed at the Yalta Conference in February 1945, Allied leaders began discussing post-war European geographical boundaries at the Tehran Conference in 1943. It was here that Roosevelt, Churchill and Stalin met for the first time, and where the latter man stealthily laid his foundations for Soviet expansion. Without the knowledge of the Polish Government in exile the 'big three' agreed in principle to the displacement of Poland, which de-facto allowed the Soviet Union to retain Polish territories earlier acquired under the Nazi-Soviet pact. However, exact borders for Poland were not openly specified by Churchill or Roosevelt for fear of alienating Poles in Britain and American citizens of Polish descent. Indeed, on 26th January 1944 Anthony Eden, British Foreign Secretary, answering questions during a House of Commons debate on the subject, flatly denied that such an agreement had taken place. Insisting instead that no border changes would be made without the free consent of the people involved. British policy, he stated, remained in accordance with the Atlantic Charter, which was signed in August 1941. This document stressed a post-war British and American commitment to the restoration of self-government for all countries with territories occupied during the war, allowing all peoples to choose their own governments.[1]

Yet by December the same year it was clear that Churchill was trying to promote the idea of a territorially restricted Poland to Members of Parliament in the House of Commons. It was unclear whether this move was designed to keep Stalin on side in case Soviet military assistance was required in the Far East campaign, or simply a recognition of British political impotence in the face of Soviet imperialistic demands. Certainly, the idea of selling Poland down the river did not go down well with Members of Parliament.

Disagreeing with Churchill's claim to be pursuing the right course of action in addressing the Polish question, Mr Raikes, MP for Essex South East protested emphatically:

We are faced with a Poland which has been devastated by years of war, a Poland which we guaranteed—though not its exact frontiers—in

Above: *Churchill, Roosevelt and Stalin pictured at the Yalta Conference in February 1945.*

1939, a Poland that is asked today to hand away practically half her territory, territory which was agreed by Russia herself under the Treaty of Riga, first in 1920 and then again in the 1930s. I could not help wondering while the Prime Minister was speaking what would have been said if, during the great days of 1940, when Britain stood alone with her honour untarnished, the one hope of civilisation in the world, any honourable or right honourable Member had got up and said 'Of course the guarantee of Poland does not mean more than that when Poland regains her liberty she will have at least half her former area. I wonder what the people of this country would have said at that time, when Polish airmen, almost alone in the nations of the world, were dying by the side of our men in the Battle of Britain, when Polish troops, alone of any troops in the world at that time, were fighting beside us on every battle front.[2]

In the weeks that followed, Raikes was not the only Member of Parliament to point out to Churchill, that plans for a restricted Poland were a complete betrayal of earlier promises. They referred him back to his rallying cry of 1940, when he claimed that:

All who have joined their causes to our own shall be restored. Freedom shall be restored to all.[3]

In theory, American and British leaders supported the Polish government in exile. Stalin however, recognized only a puppet Communist Polish Committee of Liberation based in Lublin. At Yalta it was agreed that the Lublin Committee should be expanded to include representatives of other Polish political groups, and that this organization would be recognised as a provisional government until such time as free elections could take place. This agreement was at best a ludicrously optimistic policy, and at worst a political disaster for Poland. Neither Roosevelt nor Churchill could claim to be naïve about Soviet plans for territorial expansion. In fact, when faced with Russian demands, both Roosevelt

***Above:** Bodies of dead Belgians discovered by the Allies as they advanced through Europe.*

and Churchill simply took the path of least resistance. As an American delegate at the conference observed:

It was not a question of what we would let the Russians do, but what we could get the Russians to do.[4]

Western Allied leaders agreed that Poland should be compensated for Eastern territories overrun by Soviets in 1939 but did absolutely nothing to ensure that this occurred. Subsequently Stalin reneged on his promise to hold free elections and Poland was controlled by a communist government.

Not surprisingly, at the end of the war, Polish prisoners of war in Germany felt extremely uneasy as Russians marched to liberate the camps. Lech Łaszkiewicz recalled:

When the Russians arrived, it was like a comic film. What they appeared to do was put an absolute rabble in front. They were travelling in carts with grandfather clocks and things looted away. They were blind drunk moving ahead. If they broke through then the army followed, if there were minefields, they dealt with it. There was chaos for a day or two then the Russians started to realize they had ten thousand Americans in the camp. We were let out to go into the town. It was very unsavoury. Russians were pillaging and raping; Germans were asking to take their families into the camp to protect them. We couldn't protect the women. It is one thing to fight a war, it is another to fight women and children. It's a different thing, but that's how it was. Even people in the camp were taken aback. The Russians organized guided parties outside. We asked for fresh meat, the Russians got a heard of cows into the camp! There was a big airfield nearby and the Russians were taking details from everyone. We didn't fancy this. Two RAF jeeps came, and we explained that we didn't feel safe, so the driver said jump into the jeeps with us, and that's what we did.[5]

The process of liberating German camps was not straightforward. Thousands of prisoners were riddled with diphtheria, polio or typhus. Nazi commandants had forced thousands more to march westwards, many prisoners dying by the wayside as they marched. On 27th January1945 the Soviet army liberated the purpose-built extermination camp at Auschwitz. Nothing could have prepared them for the terrible inhumanity they faced on that day. Decomposing corpses of men, women and children lay unburied in piles. Six thousand wraith-like survivors also littered the ground. The stench and filth of buildings inhabited

Above: *Emaciated survivors of a German concentration camp.*

by skeletal lice-ridden, diseased bodies was overpowering. A few weeks later a sickened BBC reporter described a similar scene when the British liberated Belsen:

> *Here over an acre of ground, lay dead and dying people. You could not see which was which except, perhaps, by a convulsive movement or the last quiver of a sigh from a living skeleton too weak to move. The*

living lay with their heads against corpses. Around them moved the awful, ghostly procession of emaciated, aimless people with nothing to do and no hope of life, unable to move out of your way and unable to look at the sights around them. This day at Belsen was the most horrible of my life.[6]

The German Commandant of Belsen had sixty thousand prisoners, fifteen thousand of which had typhus. He didn't want them to escape into the countryside and risk spreading the disease to the German population, so he contacted Allied headquarters and arranged for the British to move in ahead of time. Nurse Monica Baly accompanied the 11th Armoured Division on the first day of the liberation:

There was a temporary truce which allowed the British to take over the administration, even though the surrounding countryside was still in German hands. There was this German hospital and the mess. We thought we would have to work there, and we went inside, but the Germans had moved so quickly. There were patients still on the operating table, and bodies in the mortuary. In the officer's mess there were lunch things on the table and food on the plates. They had just walked out![7]

Camp Commandants fled for their lives for fear of being executed for war crimes. Some were never caught. Liberating members of Allied troops, shocked by what they witnessed, were never the same again. London born Major Leonard Berney was twenty-five years old when he liberated Belsen:

The sheer horror of the place was indescribable. The task before us was the like of which nobody had any knowledge or experience. What should you do when faced with 60,000 dead, sick and dying people? We were in the army to fight a war and beat the enemy. What we were suddenly thrust into was beyond anyone's comprehension.[8]

Berney later testified at the Nuremburg Trials and Camp Commandant of Belsen, Joseph Kramer, was executed.

Shocking news of the horrific holocaust filtered through to nation states across the globe. In a sense of bewilderment and numbed disbelief, the general public tried to make sense of the perverted ideology that had driven Nazi leaders and their followers to commit such atrocities. It was abundantly clear that an adherence to a sinister, eugenically motivated form of social Darwinism had propelled Germany into a moral abyss, and nowhere was this more obvious than in Poland. In total 6,000,000 Poles lost their lives, more than any other combatant nation. In Warsaw alone 700,000 were killed, more than the combined loss of British and American nationals. Polish Air Force members who lost their lives numbered 2,400.[9]

For Poles still living in Britain the immediate post-war era was extremely difficult. British people wanted to return to a pre-war normality, and over fifty per cent of the population believed that Poles should return to their own country. They were, of course, completely oblivious of what this return could mean to those who had fought for their freedom. British newspapers were suddenly full of praise for hardy Russian troops who had torn out the heart of German forces, and forcefully liberated concentration camps, forgetting the brutal Russian invasion of Poland and the tyrannical treatment of its population. Józef Jaworzyn remembered the period with painful clarity:

After the war underlies the whole story. Poles fought on other flanks, and what was being done to Poland? We Poles were not very popular. Soviet Russia was popular, and people thought we were interfering with what people thought Russia deserved. We wanted our own government and so on. It was a time of great unpopularity. Most Brits wanted Poles to go back to Poland as soon as possible. As it happened, I spent two years in hospital. In some way this made the transition easier. I was not exposed to the difficulties and hostilities of civilian life. I settled in England, but it was one of the most difficult decisions one had to take in one's life. It was also difficult to adjust from the excitement of war operations to civilian life.[10]

Bolesław Drobiński had mixed feelings after the war:

There were different emotional feelings involved. A feeling of being betrayed because we did not get our country back. Russia occupied our country and we understood that the UK and US couldn't do much, not for many people. Some went to Poland and were imprisoned, and some were shot as spies. British attitudes perhaps I understand. We had our own country. I wanted to stay in England as a British subject. I went to a Piccadilly office and filled in forms. A man told me: 'Of course you have to be permanently resident for five years.' My mother-in-law had an oil field in California. She wrote to us and wanted help with the oil business. I didn't want to go but we went. My son was born

Right: *Polish Air Force Memorial, West End Road Ruislip London.*

in 1950 and we were six years there. We returned to England and stayed. After five years I got my British citizenship.[11]

Bob Nawarski eventually managed to visit the family he was forced to leave behind in 1939:

A lot of Poles didn't go back to Poland because it was a satellite of Russia. It would mean going from one extreme to another and Russia was no friend of the Poles. You would be alright if you were a communist. It was not an option for most Poles. In mid-1946 302 Squadron was sent back to England and disbanded. I took my Spitfire to Brize Norton. I could have bought it for £50 but of course I didn't have £50, and where would I keep it? I suppose if you were a farmer and had a lot of land. Question was—what was I going to do with my civilian life? I was offered a commission in RAF with a view to making it permanent. But I was dithering because I went to university before the war. I went to a flight control school in Conningsby. I passed the course, but I knew it was only a stop gap. I was marking time more or less. In 1948 I was offered a place to do dentistry in Queens Belfast then I went to Bristol and Cardiff. I was demobbed in January 1949 and graduated in 1953.

In 1959 there was a bit of a thaw in Russian-Polish relationships, so I went back to see my parents. I hadn't seen them for twenty years. When I arrived, my father showed me a book, which had all the names of officers that were murdered by the Russians. On the train my father and I had escaped from, all the officers had been killed by Russians. A mass grave was found, which contained many thousands of Polish. Pathologists from the USA, England, Sweden and Switzerland examined the bodies and ascertained the time of death as April 1940. We knew it could not have been the Germans. People had noticed that fifteen thousand officers had just gone missing. All had been shot.

Stanisław Skalski, who was a Wing Commander and top scoring pilot was accused of being an English spy and sentenced to death. I knew him personally. His sentence was eventually commuted to life imprisonment, but they didn't tell him that. He was waiting to be executed. Would you go back to that country? My friend was shot when he went back to Poland with his Welsh wife and child. A couple of my uncles were shot in 1947 and 1949, accused of being subversives. My father said he was a railway worker. By that time, I had my English wife and there was no point in going back.[12]

It is likely that Nawarski's friend who was shot was P/O Władysław Sliwinski. When assigned to 303 Squadron Sliwinski was officially credited as destroying the 200th German aircraft. He flew with Nawarski in 302 Squadron at the time of the Normandy landings in 1944 and returned to Poland after the war with his wife and son. He was arrested and executed by the communists as an 'imperialist spy' following a show trial.

Nawarski's friend Stanisław Skalski was a legendary Polish fighter ace, renowned for being extraordinarily fearless in combat. He had entered the Battle of Britain on 27th August 1940 flying with 501 Squadron and immediately made an impact. On 5th September 1940 in combat over Canterbury he destroyed a He 111 bomber and a Me 109 escort. His Hurricane (number V664) then received a major hit from the enemy, which penetrated his fuel tank spilling burning oil all over his body. Seriously burned and with a bullet in his right femur, Skalski managed to escape the aircraft just before it burst into flames. He floated down by parachute and landed abruptly in a beetroot field. A Canadian doctor from a nearby army camp administered first aid and Skalski was then admitted to Herne Bay hospital.[13] Frustrated with boredom and desperate to get back in the air, he discharged himself prematurely from hospital to return to combat. Moreover, because the severity of his wounds prevented him from rushing to his aircraft on hearing the scramble alert, he chose to permanently sit in his cockpit waiting patiently for instructions to take-off and engage the enemy.

Skalski recovered from his wounds and went on to become the highest scoring Polish pilot of the war, with twenty-one enemy aircraft destroyed. He received Poland's highest award, the Golden Cross War Order Virtuti Militari (no. 32) and the Silver Cross Virtuti Militari (no. 8996). In addition, he was awarded with the British Distinguished Service Order and the Distinguished Flying Cross and two bars. He became the second Polish Commander of an RAF Squadron. Furthermore, his comrades in the elite Skalski's Circus emphatically stated they would follow Skalski into hell if necessary.

Skalski and his PAF comrades had fervently hoped to return to a fully restored Poland in the post-war years. This was a reasonable expectation. Their nation state had proved to be an exceptional ally; supplying crucial intelligence information to Britain, in addition to unstinting military support. Yet despite their outstanding bravery, commitment and self-sacrifice, their dreams of returning to an autonomous Poland were cruelly shattered by a mixture of political expediency and outright treachery. To add insult to injury, members

This Spitfire has been painted as the personal aircraft of Wing Commander, later Group Captain, Aleksander Gabszewicz DSO DFC who commanded No.2 Polish Fighter Wing at RAF Kirton-in-Lindsey/Church Fenton (27 Jan - 20 Jun 1943), No.1 Polish Fighter Wing at Northolt (20 Jun - 12 Dec 1943) which became No.131 Polish Wing (2nd TAF) in Oct 1943. He commanded No.18 (Polish) Sector of the 2nd TAF (25 Feb - 12 Jul 1944), and then No. 131 Polish Fighter Wing again (12 Jul 1944 - 31 May 1945).

His official PAF Victory Roll was 9½ enemy aircraft destroyed, 1 1/3 probably destroyed and 3 damaged.

The refurbishment of this aircraft was sponsored by the Polish Air Force Association

In memory of Group Captain Tom Barrett, Station Commander 2009 - 2011, a true friend of the Poles.

THIS SPITFIRE
STANDS HERE TO COMMEMORATE
THE ROLE OF
ROYAL AIR FORCE NORTHOLT
AS AN OPERATIONAL FIGHTER STATION
IN TWO WORLD WARS

Above: Memorial plaque based at the foot of a Spitfire at RAF Northolt.

of the Polish armed forces were not even allowed to take part in the 1946 London Victory Parade. This was a wholly undeserved and extreme humiliation for the Poles. In fairness to the RAF, senior personnel were very happy for members of the PAF to fly with them in the Victory Fly- past; but the Polish government in exile stated that if Polish soldiers were not allowed to march in victory parades then it would not be appropriate for Polish pilots to take part in these celebrations. Subsequently, the presence of Polish people in post-war Britain became a visible and unwelcome reminder that there were still serious problems in the world. Western politicians, along with a seemingly forgetful British public had conveniently swept aside their Polish ally. In fact, the only ally who had stood by them in their hour of greatest need.

As the British people adjusted to some form of normality at the end of the war; it was left to those who had fought and lived alongside Polish pilots to keep their memory alive. Johnny Kent was just one of hundreds of RAF airmen to extol their virtues:

> *There formed within me in those days an admiration, respect, and genuine affection for these really remarkable men which I have never lost. I formed friendships that are as firm today as they were those twenty-five years ago and I find this most gratifying. We who were privileged to fly and fight with them will never forget, and Britain must never forget how much she owes to the loyalty, indomitable spirit and sacrifice of these Polish fliers. They were our staunchest Allies in our darkest days, may they always be remembered as such![14]*

Poland finally became free of communist rule in 1989. A few years later Queen Elizabeth II, who had lived through the grimmest days of the war, gently reminded British people of the debt they owed to the Polish Few:

> *As our two countries fought together against tyranny, I remember the Polish anthem being played each week on the BBC along with those of our other gallant allies. And we will never forget, in my country, the courage of Polish pilots, part of the Few, to whom Churchill rightly said so much was owed. If Poland had not stood with us in those days, who knows—the candle of freedom might have been snuffed out. The Poles who stayed in Britain founded a community which has given much to our national life. But their freedom was not reflected in their own country Zeby Polska była Polska. (Let Poland be Poland).[15]*

Chapter 11
Franciszek Kornicki

To illustrate the role of the PAF in wartime Britain, the voices of many individual pilots have been quoted throughout this book. Each of them had their own extraordinary story to tell. The following is the story of just one ordinary Polish pilot, but it is representative of thousands of his comrades in arms.

In 2017 the RAF Museum at Hendon held a public vote to select a representative 'ordinary' pilot to be profiled next to a Spitfire Mk V. From a choice of a dozen or so, of various nationalities and backgrounds, Franciszek Kornicki was the winner by a massive majority. Upon hearing this momentous news, he was surprised and a little bewildered, humbly pointing out that he was just one of a great many who helped to win the war.[1] He was also quick to give credit to his ground crew:

My aircraft was cared for by a fitter and a rigger—great chaps—and my only regret is that I cannot recall their names, because they deserve equal recognition for everything this wonderful aircraft achieved.[2]

Kornicki began his flying career in 1936 at the Polish Air Force (PAF) College in Dęblin and described the curriculum there as being very similar to that of Cranwell. His previous experience of flying gliders, along with a natural talent for mathematics, were valuable assets for pilot training. In 1939 he was posted to a PAF base eight hundred kilometres south of Warsaw, and stoically fought against the German invasion:

Luftwaffe had the numerical advantage and better equipment. We had problems with aircraft. There were often blockages in the guns of Polish aircraft, so we came back to airfields—it was a disaster. On one occasion an Me 109 got onto a pilot just about to land, he arrived before attack. Three chaps coming back tried to intervene, trying to circle round; he landed safely but was killed later. The PAF was not strategic. Fighter wing was parcelled between armies; we should have attacked in numbers, not bits and pieces. Within first four days of

Left: Young Franciszek Kornicki.

> *Germans bombing—they were roaring forward, PAF was successful at night. But there were not enough anti-tank weapons. Out of my entry (college class) a quarter of chaps flying light bombers were shot down. It was a disaster in every respect. But no matter what some history books might say, in spite of the situation, losses inflicted on the Luftwaffe were considerable. A friend of mine saw a column of Polish vehicles being attacked by German planes, he shot both of them down. We didn't give up. Observation rooms were reporting ten to twenty-five enemy aircraft coming in raid after raid. I went to the hospital, it was covered with wounded, it was a nightmare.[3]*

When it became clear that Polish forces were completely overwhelmed by the invading German Blitzkrieg, Kornicki teamed up with two friends and travelled in an Opel car across the border into Romania. Being a clever and astute man, he compiled a dictionary of basic words in different languages, for future use:

> *There was a woman standing on the border with some apples. She spoke Ukrainian and I could speak Ukrainian. I ask her 'What is the word for bread? What is butter etc?' A few kilometres away there was a woman with milk. Later on, I used some German. I carried on with my dictionary because the Romanians spoke French. We arrived at a military post and asked a young Romanian soldier, 'Can we avoid going to camp? We have car and money can you help?' He looked after us, but he wanted a motorbike. We were sent across the Danube, but we were arrested mid-Danube; then we tried again. Chief of police was a very nice man who gave us the address of his own tailor and helped us get civilian clothes. There was a Treaty between the French and Romanians and police chief gave us a policeman to help us cross the river. We left him there with money. Arrived at Bucharest Embassy and they produced passports on foolscap paper. We had to queue for photos. Impossible to get exit visa from Romania. They had set up a Home Office team to revoke visas from Poles. We went to port where there was a Greek ship called Patris. Passports said we were agricultural students. You could bribe anyone in Romania. Embarkations took place at night. I got someone else's passport, put my collar up. I had fifteen minutes to learn details on passport. We went via Black Sea, Dardanelles and Malta. Four of us stayed in a bathroom full of pillows! Quite by chance I tried to push one door on the boat, then a little bit more, and we secured a lot of pillows. A lot of fellows were delighted to*

Above: *Franciszek Kornicki pictured with his aircraft.*

get a pillow. From Malta we went to Marseilles where French ladies
greeted us with a nice welcome and a little parcel. We thought France
will fight but we were mistaken.[4]

As German Panzer Divisions subsequently trampled across France, a
disillusioned Kornicki and his friends gathered on the coast to await a sea
passage to Britain. They were unable to collect any of their belongings and
could make no attempt to get airborne. Guards had been placed around aircraft
bases to prevent the commandeering of French planes by Poles and Czechs.
Evacuation trains were frequently diverted, and ships such as the Arandora Star
were sent to several ports as part of Operation Ariel. Furthermore, regardless
of orders issued to French officers to detain members of Polish forces, no sane
Frenchman was likely to take on a large cohort of fighting men intent on leaving
the country. Kornicki recalled:

Left: *These two crucifixes were wired into the cockpit of Franciszek Kornicki's Spitfire by his rigger and fitter.*

> *There were masses of us, and we were armed. A French General told us 'You cannot leave France. These are my orders! You are all interned.' Our Army chaps replied, 'You say to go to camp. We say we go to Arandora Star. We all go to sail away.' Half-way across we picked up a German radio message to say Arandora Star was sunk. We had lots of laughs about it.[5]*

Upon arrival in Liverpool Polish airmen were taken by buses to a race- course in Cheshire. Hundreds of tents had been erected in readiness, and rudimentary beds were constructed of straw. Each tent contained one copy of 'Teach Yourself English,' and food consisted mainly of bread, corned beef and vegetables. Everything was very organized, and surroundings were favourable:

> *My first impressions—we saw a lot of well-built houses with gardens and flowers. I thought what a nice country this is, I remember thinking that. Language was difficult so we struggled. I found that 'u' could be pronounced in ten different ways. When we left camp to go to the Air Force base in Blackpool—we found it was completely taken over by Poles. It was summer so visitors everywhere. Lots of girls helped us with the language, which was kind of them. In a matter of fact, I corresponded with one. I said: 'I will write to you in broken English and you can send back with corrections.' We went to Winter Gardens' dances and treated young girls properly. Language problem was serious at first posting with 307 Squadron on Defiants. An operational dictionary was devised—height angel 15,000 feet and speed. There were different expressions for formation. Tally-Ho (spotting enemy and point of attack), enemy aircraft above and enemy aircraft below. A short dictionary but sufficient. When it came to encounters with the enemy, we started in English but in the excitement of battle we would return back to Polish. It was quicker. 'Look out Jerry on your tail,' it was easier*

to say it in Polish. We never said 'Tally-Ho.' We said, 'We attack!'
Sometimes we used the clock and said '3, o'clock Jerries;' never a long
verbal explanation, as quick as possible. There was no time for
procedures, you just said what came into your head.[6]

High scoring Polish Squadrons gained fearsome reputations, prompting some
members of the press to claim that the Poles were violent by nature. This
spurious assumption was refuted by Kornicki:

It is difficult to take a wholesale view and say that every Pole is
particularly aggressive. In any group of men there are different types.
Men who were born killers were often a nuisance in formation. They
would peel off looking for individual success. A Squadron is a
formation that should fight together and after a fight get together again.
There are fighters, and there are observers, who fight to defend
themselves, but they are not keen. Then there are cards everywhere. We
had our own reasons to dislike the Germans.[7]

When questioned about feelings during combat he was equally candid:

You have a mixture of emotions. It depends if you are in a good
position. If you are attacking you are elated, you are excited, you are
feeling good. But if you are being jumped upon you have to defend
yourself, you have to make sure you survive. It's a different story. You
are looking after number one first of all and sticking to formation as
far as possible. There were occasions for example when Squadrons
were attacked by several German fighters, twice or three times the
number of them. They defended themselves very successfully by forming
a circle. Squadron Commander was a very clever man and said: 'we
can't fight against them so we will form a circle.' Germans tried to
attack but it wasn't so easy; because if someone attacked one person
then the one behind may have the opportunity to fire a short burst, that
was useful. The circle could go right down to the ground and attack
would end on the ground.[8]

Following his brief posting to 307 Squadron Kornicki was moved to Leconfield
to join the high scoring 303 Squadron, he then became a member of 315
Squadron. Almost nineteen months later, at the tender age of twenty-six
Kornicki became the youngest Polish Squadron Commander when he took
command of 308 Squadron. Although he pointed out that:

In comparison to other pilots in the Battle of Britain I was an old man.
There were pilots aged eighteen and nineteen flying and dying.[9]

Soon after his promotion however, Kornicki suffered a burst appendix at 25,000 feet. To some extent, gastro-intestinal problems were an occupational hazard for pilots but a burst appendix which, left untreated, resulted in extensive peritonitis, was a potentially fatal condition.[10]

Initially, the young Squadron Commander assumed that he just had stomach-ache:

I was over France leading 308 Squadron, doing a sweep over northern France with another Squadron. We were operational but not doing much. We were parading, making sure we were noticed, if they come up to interfere with us then we would fight, but nobody did. At one point I felt a sharp pain in my tummy. I didn't understand what was happening, so I checked the oxygen was on. I stayed with the Squadron back to Northolt, went to the mess, had tea and felt easier. I went to the cinema with a couple of chaps and asked to see the medical officer when I got back. He stuck a finger in my tummy, and I yelled! He said, 'This is appendix.' There were no surgery facilities and the appendix had burst so I was sent to hospital. Friends came to see me after the operation and told me lots of jokes; but it was painful for me to laugh. I told them to talk about funerals from now on. Two friends, Monica and Mary, came to see me in the hospital, but the civilian nurses didn't like it. They said they could only stay for five minutes. I complained to the sister and said they should be allowed to stay longer—besides, I told the sister I was engaged to both of them![11]

Mary and Monica joined the Air Transport Auxiliary (ATA) and trained as pilots. This was the nearest women could hope to get in terms of wartime flying with the RAF or PAF. Nonetheless, their work was very important, and they were highly respected by their male comrades. Three Polish women were among the ATA, including the daughter of Marshal Józef Pilsudski, who effectively ruled Poland (albeit unofficially) between 1926 until his death in 1935.

Kornicki meanwhile, made a full recovery and was then posted to command 317 Squadron. In August 1943, while fulfilling bomber escort duties over Northern France, Kornicki kept the Squadron in position until enemy fighters had committed themselves to a diving attack. He then ordered the Squadron to

Right: *Franciszek Kornicki with his rigger on the aircraft wing (name unknown), and his fitter Cpl. Mirczyslaw Kubalski cowling above them on the fuselage.*

turn around and mount a climbing attack on the enemy. In the course of the engagement, four enemy aircraft were destroyed for no loss. Returning then to England at tree-top height, the Squadron in line abreast, they shot at any target of opportunity as they roared over Northern France. In retrospect Kornicki stated:

> *It may not have done much to advance the war effort, but it was fantastic for morale.*[12]

He was then awarded Poland's highest military honour: the Virtuti Militari, for this engagement and his courageous, exemplary leadership.

Characteristically, along with calm, perceptive leadership qualities, and superb, instinctive flying skills, Kornicki possessed an abundant sense of humour. He cheekily played tricks on his friends, immediately grasped the funny side of various, seemingly dire situations, and shared numerous jokes in the mess. A sense of humour provided an ideal antidote to the intensity of aerial combat. Social outings also helped to relieve stress. He recalled being invited to attend 'proper balls,' and weekly dances in a huge gymnasium with hundreds of people weaving around. These were arranged by the Station Commander's wife and were great fun. Other methods of relaxation included playing cards or snooker in the mess, reading or listening to music, and having a drink in the bar:

> *In Northolt at one time there were lovely sessions where the Station Commander used to play a violin in the ladies' room. He used to put a bottle of scotch on the table and when it was gone, we'd get another. We all went to the cinema very frequently it was a great distraction. At the Orchard hotel in Uxbridge there were a lot of girls and romances. I think the proprietor had a private line to Northolt, because he would commiserate or give congratulations when we went in. We had £15 a month and paid £5 for extra messing. Towards the end of the month we would be broke. But if we went to the Orchard and paid a shilling for a pint of beer, we made it last. The proprietor would notice, and come over with another pint for you, on the house. Always at the end of the evening British and Polish national anthems were played. The whole of Uxbridge knew what the Polish national anthem sounded like!*
>
> *Ground crew were always making jokes. When a pilot had to visit another Polish Squadron Station (never on pleasure allegedly), ground crew, once they knew, would write several messages on your aircraft. Some were funny, some rude, some general messages. I had graffiti on my Spitfire, one message would say: 'Hi chaps, how are you? Greetings on the propeller!'*[13]

Sometimes however practical jokes could be taken a step too far. Prior to Polish Squadrons moving in 1943 to Perranporth in Cornwall for example, Canadian airmen had warned the local community of the incoming 'dangerous Poles.' Thus, after the Canadians had left Perranporth Polish pilots were systematically ignored by the locals:

We had some amusing things happen with Canadians and we inherited planes from them—they were in a terrible state. Well, anyway we got that sorted out. The focal point for social life was the Stork Club. A lot of people evacuated from London and other places lived in Perranporth. We went to the Stork Club the first night we were free, and nobody would talk to us. We said we want beer and we got beer, then everyone turned their backs on us. We were very surprised. We took our beer and went into the garden. We thought we will try again tomorrow, so we tried again, and the same thing happened. We thought if they choose to ignore us, we'll ignore them. Eventually one lady said: 'Look you might think this is very odd that we ignore you; but we were warned that every Pole carried a knife and every girl would be raped and all that!' I said, 'And you believed them?' (laughs) She said, 'Well what else could we do, we didn't know.' We knew that this was a Canadian prank, but we didn't think it was very fair of them to do this. Anyway, after that everything was fine.[14]

Although a naturally humble man, there was no doubt that Kornicki was exceptionally talented in the air. With remarkable intelligence and stealth, he was adept at predicting the actions of enemy pilots:

On one occasion there was a general melee and I found myself taking evading action. Suddenly everyone had disappeared. I was flying quietly, looking back all the time. Then I spotted a German aircraft stalking me from above. I thought, he will catch me in the end, so the only thing I could do was fox him somehow. The thing I did—I applied the rudder and tail control in such a way that I would drift. It would appear to him that I was flying straight. I was actually drifting all the time. I waited until he started firing so I would see the traces, and that's what happened. The traces were a few yards from my left wing, a good burst of a gun. I immediately turned right, and I knew that he would overshoot, so I turned left. There we were, he could see there was no future in it, and he went down. I thought fine, I'll get home, and I did. Several things like this happened.[15]

As the war progressed and Allied bomber offensives increased Kornicki was highly critical of overall planning. Recalling this period, he spoke passionately about the unnecessary loss of life:

> *There were all sorts of operations, some of them ill thought out and too expensive in aircraft and lives. 315 Squadron went once, with another Squadron; with six little bombs escorting six Hurricanes to bomb a target near Calais, attacking from low level. Well this place was full of guns from every calibre, so of course the six Hurricanes went down and four of our chaps went down. Squadron above was alright. What was achieved? Nothing! What did the planners think about? I don't know, because this was a mad, mad, example of bad operations. They would order things like attacks on ships. Well the Germans had gunships. They were bristling with guns. To attack those guns was a very dicey business. Doing that of course, the aircraft who could do that effectively were the Typhoons with rockets. But to send a Spitfire there was madness, because the 20mm guns and 303 machine guns could kill a chap if he was in the way, but they couldn't do any damage to the ship. This was again very bad planning. In every war in every time there are good planners and bad planners, so there you are. The people on the receiving end have to carry out those orders.[16]*

When asked his opinion with regard to the post war political situation Kornicki described the roller coaster of emotions experienced by all Poles:

> *We were full of hope after the Battle of Britain. Eventually we knew we couldn't lose. Once Germany attacked Russia. Great Britain never lost in war anyhow—not an important war anyhow (laughs). We were full of hope and building our Air Force. We had ten fighter and four bomber Squadrons, and a lot of people in industry in technical establishments getting ready to return to Poland, with small, organized, efficient Air Force. Main damage was done in Tehran. Stalin was in such a strong position that he could say what he wanted and do what he wanted. My feeling is that the Allies—USA did not take advantage of the earlier situation to extract obligations from them (the Russians) for the post war state of Europe. The hopes of Poles were completely dashed.[17]*

Certainly, this was a valid criticism of political proceedings between the USA and Russia. When Stalin was constantly demanding that Western Allies open a Second Front to alleviate pressure on Russian troops, the USA may well have been able to secure promises from Stalin. It is unlikely however, that Stalin would have honoured such guarantees elicited under a temporary duress. In a post war political climate that quickly descended into the Cold War, Poland was totally dominated by communist rule. This was a terrible tragedy. As the British Ambassador correctly observed:

Poles are interested in three things—past, present and future. They have a love of their country and a love of freedom.[18]

Like many of his contemporaries Franciszek Kornicki decided to stay in Britain once the war was over. In 1948 he married Patience Williams; in the same year a beautiful memorial dedicated to honour and commemorate the Polish Airmen who lost their lives in the Second World War, was unveiled at South Ruislip in the London Borough of Hillingdon. Engraved on the monument are the following words:

I HAVE FOUGHT A GOOD FIGHT.
I HAVE FINISHED MY COURSE.
I HAVE KEPT THE FAITH

2 Timothy 4:7[19]

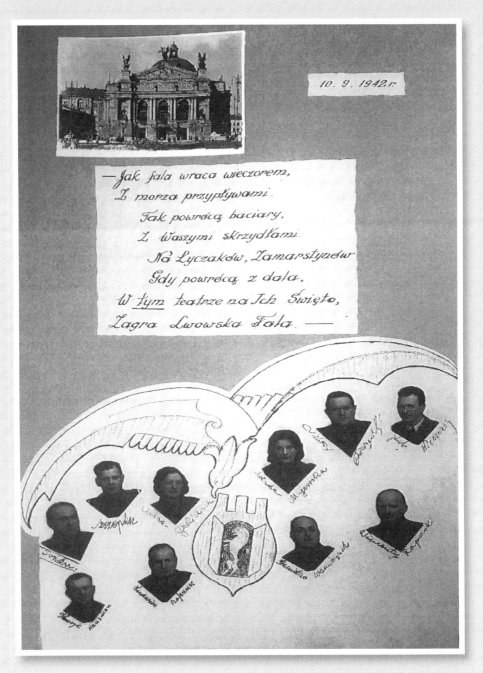

This is artwork compiled by members of 307 squadron
on the second anniversary of their formation.

References

Chapter 1: Journeys to Britain

1 Overy, R., The Origins of the Second World War, 1987 p.61. See also newer edition published in 1998.

2 Chamberlain. N., Hansard House of Commons Parliamentary Debates 5th Series 31st March 1939, vol 345 col 2415-20

3 Major General Sir Alfred Knox., Hansard House of Commons Parliamentary Debates 5th Series 7th September 1939, vol 351 col 578-87

4 Ibid

5 Łaszkiewicz, Lech, Stanisław., Oral History Testimony, Imperial War Museum Sound Archives, catalogue reference   12909

6 Ibid

7 Jaworzyn, Joseph, Franciszek Oral History Testimony, Imperial War Museum Sound Archives, catalogue reference 18830

8 Drobinski, Boleslaw, Henryk., Oral History Testimony, Imperial War Museum Sound Archives, catalogue reference 12892

9 Nawarski, Bob., Oral History Testimony, Imperial War Museum Sound Archives, catalogue reference 27237

10 Jaworzyn, Joseph, Franciszek, Oral History Testimony, Imperial War Muscum Sound Archives, catalogue reference 18830

11 Krzystek, Tadeusz, Jerzy, Oral History Testimony, Imperial War Museum Sound Archives, catalogue reference 10618

12 Łaszkiewicz, Lech, Stanisław, Oral History Testimony, Imperial War Museum Sound Archives catalogue reference 12909

13 Jaworzyn, Joseph, Franciszek, Oral History Testimony, Imperial War Museum Sound Archives catalogue reference 18830

14 The fate of RMS Lancastria was suppressed until after the war. The disaster represents the largest loss of life in British maritime history.

15 Nawarski, Bob, Oral History Testimony, Imperial War Museum Sound Archives catalogue reference 27237

16 Ibid

17 Jaworzen, Joseph, Franciszek, Oral History Interview, Imperial War Museum Sound Archives, catalogue reference 18830

Chapter 2: Organization and Training

1 Churchill, Winston, Hansard House of Commons Parliamentary Debates, 5th Series 18th June 1940 vol 362 col 51-64

2 Falconer, J., Royal Air Force Technical Innovations Manual (2017)

3 Range and direction finding, RDF was later called RADAR—Radio Detection and Ranging. Chain Home was operational by September 1938.

4 Kornicki, R. Information supplied to author via email correspondence.

5 Nawarski, Bob, Oral History Testimony Imperial War Museum Sound Archives catalogue reference: 27237

6 Jaworzyn, Joseph, Franciszek, Oral History Testimony Imperial War Museum Sound Archives catalogue reference 18830

7 Ibid

8 Ibid

9 Drobinski, Boleslaw, Henryk, Oral History Testimony Imperial War Museum Sound Archives catalogue reference 12892

10 Hale, C.A., memoirs of 307 Squadron 10th September 1940-10th September 1942. Exeter Record Offices reference: 7931Z

11 Kent, J., One of the Few (2008) pp. 90-91

12 Kornicki, R., Information supplied to author via email correspondence.

13 Nawarski, Bob, Oral History Testimony Imperial War Museum Sound Archives catalogue reference 27237

14 Krzystek, Tadeusz, Jerzy, Oral History Testimony Imperial War Museum Sound Archives catalogue reference 10618

15 Nawarski, Robert, Oral History Testimony Imperial War Museum Sound Archives catalogue reference 27237

16 Drobinski, Boleslaw, Henryk, Oral History Testimony Imperial War Museum Sound Archives catalogue reference 12892

17 Kellett, R, G., Skrzydla Nr 106/592 quoted in Pemberton, L., 303 Kosciuszko Squadron, pamphlet produced to accompany the Memorial Service held on 30th August 2014 for Wing Commander Ronald Gustave Kellett, Commanding Officer of 303 Squadron during the Battle of Britain.

18 Falconer, J., RAF 100, 1918-2018: Technical Innovations Manual (Haynes Publishing 2017) p. 108-109

19 Jaworzyn, Joseph, Franciszek, Oral History Testimony Imperial War Museum Sound Archives catalogue reference 18830

20 Urbanowicz, W., Dawn of Victory, Znak, Cracow, 2009, quoted in Sikora, P., The Polish Few 2018 p. 55-56

Chapter 3: The Battle of Britain Phases One, Two and Three

1 cia.gov/library: German Plans for the Invasion of Britain, item 20B., p 14-15. See also National Archives Hitler's War Directive no.16 ref: LCO/67/71

2 The diary of George Gibbs—Lord Mayors' Secretary and Deputy to Mr. M Webb, Bristol's Air Raid Precautions Controller. Bristol Record Office reference: 39735/Bri/IM/H/1/13

3 Frantisek, Josef scored a total of 17 kills and one probable in September 1940.

4 Nicholson, J., Flight Lieutenant was the only pilot in Fighter Command to be awarded the Victoria Cross. This act of valour occurred on 16th August 1940 near the coast of Southampton.

5 Ostowicz, Antoni was the first Polish pilot to be killed in the Battle of Britain, shot down near Swanage on 11th August 1940 by a Messershmitt Bf 109

6 Kent, J., One of the Few (2008) p. 91-92

7 Ibid p. 92

8 Ibid p. 93

9 National Archives Air50/117/14

10 Ibid

11 National Archives Air/50/117/74 Intelligence Fighter Command Combat Report compiled by E. M. Hadwin reference: FC/S 17570/Intelligence., p.90., dated: 29.9.40. Please note that Hadwin is also spelt Hdawen or Hadwan in some official reports.

12 Ibid

13 Ibid

14 Kent, J., One of the Few (2008) p.93

Chapter 4: Battle of Britain Phases Four and Five

1 Starns, P., Blitz Hospital: true stories of nursing in wartime London. (2018) pp.44-45.

2 Severe aerial bombardment of London continued until 10th May 1941

3 Richards, D., Official History of the Royal Air Force 1939-1945 (1953) pp. 183-184

4   National Archive reference: AIR/50/117/10

5   Drobinski, Boleslaw Henryk., Oral History Testimony, Imperial War
    Museum Sound Archive catalogue reference 12899. Please note that
    Drobinski is recalling the story of Sgt Ryszard Gorecki, which occurred
    in the summer of 1941. Information supplied by Wojtek Matusiak.

6   National Archives reference AIR/27-1655-(2)

7   Kowalski, J, R., Nad ujsciem Tamizy (Over the Thames Estuary), Skrzydla
    Wings, no. 120/606 quoted in Sikora, P., The Polish Few (2016) pp. 162-
    163.

8   Sikora, P., The Polish Few (2016) p. 167

9   National Archive reference AIR/50/117/2

10 National Archive reference AIR/50/117/14

11 Ibid

12 Baly M., 'Royal College of Nursing History of Nursing Journal,' vol. 3
    (1990), pp. 58-59

13 National Archives reference AIR/27-1655(2)

14 Bristol Record Office reference: 39735/BRI.IM/1/13

15 Ibid

16 National Archive reference AIR/50/117/2

17 National Archive reference AIR/50/117/14

18 National Archive reference AIR/50/117/14

19 Sikora, P., The Polish Few (2016) p.176

20 Kent, J., One of the Few (2000) p. 105

21 Ibid preface written by Air Chief Marshall Sir Keith Park

22 Ibid p. 111

23 During the Battle of Britain one hundred and forty-five Polish pilots flew
    in defence of Britain. Seventy-nine of these were sprinkled around
    British RAF Squadrons, thirty-two flew in the Polish 302 Squadron and
    thirty-four in the Polish 303 Squadron. Flying Officer Witold
    Urbanowicz scored fifteen kills. The top scoring pilot was
    Czechoslovakian born Josef Frantisek with 17 kills to his name.

Chapter 5: The Blitz

1   Churchill, W., Speech given at the Mansion House London 9th November

2   Starns, P., Blitz Families: the children who stayed behind (2012) p. 121.

3   Drobinski, Boleslaw Henryk, Oral History Testimony Imperial War Museum
    Sound Archives catalogue reference: 12899

4   'British Journal of Nursing' November 1940, p185

5 National Archives AIR/27/1655/4

6 Curnock, G. C., Hospitals Under Fire (1941) pp78-82

7 National Archives Air/50/118/49 Fighter Command Report from No. 11 Group to Fighter Command H.Q. detailing patrol of 306 Squadron 17th June 1941. Please note that names in the text differ from those in the original report. This is because names were spelt incorrectly in the original report. Names in the text are correct according to information supplied by Wojtek Matusiak.

8 National Archives Air/50/117/102 Fighter Command Report from No. 12 Group to Fighter Command H.Q. detailing patrol of 303 Squadron 18th June 1941.

9 National Archives Air/50/117/14

10 Ibid

11 Nawarski, Bob., Oral History Testimony Imperial War Museum Sound Archives catalogue number 27237

12 Budzik, Kazimierz., Oral History Testimony Imperial War Museum Sound Archives catalogue number 12135

Chapter 6: The Ground Crew

1 Nawarski, Bob., Oral History Testimony Imperial War Museum Sound Archives catalogue reference 27237

2 Fiedler, A., Squadron 303 The Story of a Polish Fighter Squadron with the RAF (1943) pp. 125-126

3 Marsh, G., Squadron 303, Kosciuszko, The Collaboration with the English quoted in Sikora, P., The Polish Few (2016) p. 178

4 Hale, C. A. F/Lt. 10.9.1940, Exeter Record Office reference: 7931Z

5 White, G., Letter dated 10th December 1942 to Wing Commander Michalowski thanking him for the inscribed Polish Night Fighter song is held at Exeter Record Office, also included in the History of Bristol at War.

6 Budzik K., Oral History Testimony Imperial War Museum Sound Archives catalogue reference 12135

7 Nawarski, Bob., Oral History Testimony Imperial War Museum Sound Archives catalogue reference 27237

8 Imperial War Museum Documents Archives catalogue reference 14379

9 Ibid

10 This quarantine was necessary because of epidemics of typhus and other diseases.

11 Babicz, T., In War and Peace: collected memories of Birmingham's Poles (2011)

12 Armitage, M., Air Chief Vice Marshall., 'The Polish Apprentices at Halton' in: Royal Air Force Historical Society Journal no. 36 (2006) pp. 43-51 Based on original Polish source material provided by Eugene Borysiuk (709020)

13 National Archives Foreign and Allied Forces Code B, 92 reference: AIR/2/8202

14 National Archives AIR/24/1530. Polish women were also recruited in France following the D-Day invasion, see: National Archives WO/219/4913

15 National Archives AIR/20/1371 1943-1945

16 Armitage, M., Air Chief Marshall., 'The Polish Apprentices at Halton' in: Royal Air Force Historical Society Journal no. 36 (2006) pp. 43-51 Based on original Polish source material provided by Eugene Borysiuk (709020)

17 Ibid

18 Aircraftsman Antoni Rossochacki was killed on 27th October 1940 while Squadron was resting. It was important for pilots and ground crew to have rest periods in between periods of intense fighting.

19 Marsh, G., Squadron 303, Kosciuszko, 'The Collaboration with the English' quoted in Sikora, P., The Polish Few (2016) pp. 179-180

20 Imperial War Museum Documents Archives catalogue references: LBY E.J. 2444., LBY E.J. 5259., & LBY E. J. 4318

21 Park, Keith., quoted in preface of Kent, J., One of the Few (2008)

22 Starns, P., BBC Radio4 Frontline Females Vol 1 See also: Starns, P., Combat Medicine (2019)

23 Ibid

24 Nawarski, Bob., Oral History Testimony Imperial War Museum Sound Archives catalogue reference: 27237 In this extract Nawarski is referring to RAF/PAF fighter/bomber missions of 1944.

Chapter 7: The Night Owls

1 F/Lt. Hale, C. A., Memoirs 10th September 1940-10th September 1941 Exeter Record Offices reference: 7931Z

2 For more information on these raids please consult Wasley, G., Blitz: An Account of Hitler's Aerial War Over Plymouth in March 1991 and the Events that followed (1991) See also Starns, P., Blitz Families: the

children who stayed behind. (2012)

3 Budzik, K., Oral History Testimony Imperial War Museum Sound Archives catalogue reference: 12135. Please note that Budzik was a day fighter and did not serve with 307 Squadron. In the quoted extract he is describing his training in night flying techniques.

4 National Archives Air/81/4430, Air/81/4663 & Air/81/5170 respectively.

5 F/Lt. Hale, C. A., memoirs 10th September 1940- 10th September 1941 Exeter Record Offices reference: 7931Z

6 Letter dated 24th November 1941, held at Exeter Record Office reference: 7931Z

7 F/Lt. Hale, C. A., Memoirs 10th September 1940-10th September 1941 Exeter Record Offices reference: 7931Z

8 Daily Sketch, 6th August 1942 p.1.

9 Dalton, H., Letter written to Wing Commander Jan Michalowski dated 4th September 1942. By this stage the Eagle Owls had adopted the insignia of the Owl and had taken to using the hooting call of an owl to greet each other.

10 This flag was lost after the war, but thanks to research conducted by Michael Parrott in Exeter, a new flag was presented to Exeter's mayor in 2012 and November 15th is now commemorated as 307 Squadron Day every year.

11 Poem written on the 12th August 1942 by a lady called Betty to a gentleman of the 307 Squadron who Betty refers to as Jashu. Exeter Record Offices reference: 7931Z

12 Goddard, K., Letter to Wing Commander Jan Michalowski thanking him for organising fund-raising concerts, dated 19th February 1943. Exeter Record Offices reference: 7931Z

Chapter 8: Circuses, Rhubarbs, Rodeos and Ramrods

1 Sikora, P., The Polish Few (2016) p.183

2 Jaworzyn, J., Oral History Testimony, Imperial War Museum Sound Archives catalogue reference: 18830

3 Budzik, K, Oral History Testimony, Imperial War Museum Sound Archives catalogue reference: 12135

4 National Archives AIR/50/127 Personal Combat Report Sgt. Brzeski dated 14th July 1941

5 Ibid Personal Combat Report Flight Sergeant Brzeski dated 8th November 1941.

6 Harris, A, T., Head of Bomber Command, Speech given to the general public in March 1942

7 RAF Museum website accessed 1/10/2019

8 Nawarski, Bob., Oral History Testimony Imperial War Museum Sound Archives catalogue reference: 27237

9 Budzik K., Oral History Testimony, Imperial War Museum Sound Archives catalogue reference: 12135

10 Rigden, D., SOE Syllabus: Lessons in Ungentlemanly Warfare (2004), p.192

11 Bines, J., 'The Polish Country Section of the Special Operations Executive 1940-1946: a British perspective,' unpublished Ph.D. thesis University of Stirling (2008)

12 National Archives AIR/50/127 Personal Combat Report Flight Sergeant Brzeski dated 25th April 1942

13 National Archives AIR/50/127 Personal Combat Report Flight Sergeant Brzeski dated 26th July 1942

14 National Archives AIR/50/454/2 Secret Wing Intelligence Combat Report Northolt (Polish) Wing Ramrod S.36 Part II 6th September 1943.

15 Nawarski, Bob., Oral History Testimony Imperial War Museum Sound Archives catalogue reference: 27237

16 Kitchen, M., A World in Flames (1990) p.136

Chapter 9: D-Day and beyond

1 Nawarski, Bob., Oral History Testimony Imperial War Museum Sound Archives catalogue reference: 27237

2 Budzik, K., Oral History Testimony Imperial War Museum Sound Archives catalogue reference: 12135

3 Kirchner, W., quoted in: Kornicki, R., Plumetot 1944: The Return of the Polish Air Force to the Mainland of Europe (2019) p.4

4 Starns, P., Frontline Females BBC Radio4 broadcast April 1998

5 Łaszkiewicz, L., Oral History Testimony Imperial War Museum Sound Archives catalogue reference: 12909

6 Ibid

7 Ibid

8 Kornicki, R., Plumetot 1944: The Return of the Polish Air Force to the Mainland of Europe (2019) p.11

9 Dowling, A., Janek: a story of survival (1989) p.163

10 Lyne, H. L., Imperial War Museum Documents Archive reference: 7008. Sgt Lyne was shot down and spent the remainder of the

war in Stalag Luft (Barth).

11   Ibid p.167

12   Walker, A., Oral History Testimony Imperial War Museum Sound Archives catalogue reference: 17977/2/1-2

13   Neal, D., Interview given to BBC West 21st November 2010

14   Bristol Record Office reference: 44891/3/41 A Service of Memorial takes place at All Saints Church Long Ashton Bristol every time 21st November falls on Christ the King Day. The next Memorial Service will therefore be held in 2021.

15   Daily Mirror 12th December 1944.

16   Krzystek T., Oral History Testimony Imperial War Museum Sound Archives catalogue reference: 10618

17   Drobinski, B., Oral History Testimony Imperial War Museum Sound Archives catalogue reference: 12892

18   Budzik, K., Oral History Testimony Imperial War Museum Sound Archives catalogue reference: 12135

19   Overy, R., Why the Allies Won (1995) p. 176

20   Nawarski, Bob., Oral History Testimony Imperial War Museum Sound Archives catalogue reference 27237. In this extract Nawarski recalls events out of sequence. Tented accommodation was available at Plumetot but at Ghent pilots and ground crew were housed in properly constructed buildings.

21   Information supplied by Wojtek Matusiak and Richard Kornicki, email correspondence with author 6th January 2020.

22   Krzystek T., Oral History Testimony Imperial War Museum Sound Archives catalogue reference: 10618

Chapter 10: The legacy

1   Eden, A., Hansard House of Commons Parliamentary Debates 5th Series 26th January 1944, vol.396, col:663-665

2   Raikes, MP Essex South East, addressing Churchill, W., Hansard House of Commons Parliamentary Debates 5th Series 15th December 1944, vol. 406 col: 1478-1578

3   Churchil, W., Hansard House of Commons Parliamentary Debates 5th Series 18th June 1940, vol 362, col 51-64

4   Byrnes, J.F., American delegate to the Yalta conference speaking in February 1945, he was subsequently promoted to US Secretary of State.

5 Łaszkiewicz, L., Oral History Testimony Imperial War Museum Sound Archives catalogue reference: 12909

6 BBC Broadcast 15th April 1945

7 Baly, M. quoted from Starns, P., Frontline Females BBC Radio4 vol. 2

8 Berney, L., Extract from his obituary: The Independent 8th March 2016

9 Statistics obtained from the Polish Air Force Memorial Committee website.

10 Jaworzyn, J., Oral History Testimony Imperial War Museum Sound Archives catalogue reference 18830

11 Drobinski, B., Oral History Testimony Imperial War Museum Sound Archive catalogue reference 12892

12 Nawarski, Bob., Oral History Testimony Imperial War Museum Sound Archives catalogue reference 27237

13 National Archives AIR/81/3228

14 Kent. J., quoted in Sikora, P., The Polish Few (2016) p.278

15 Her Majesty Queen Elizabeth II speaking in the Polish Parliament 26th March 1996

Chapter 11: Franciszek Kornicki

1 The Telegraph 21st September 2017

2 Ibid

3 Kornicki, F., Oral History Testimony Imperial War Museum Sound Archives catalogue reference: 028594

4 Ibid

5 Ibid

6 Ibid

7 Ibid

8 Ibid

9 Ibid

10 As outlined by Boyles Law, the increased abdominal pressure caused by flying at altitude frequently caused physical problems, usually these were minor and temporary. In addition, pilots often experienced neck problems, this was due to the constant need to move their heads to remain vigilant within the confined cockpit space. For further information please see Starns, P., Combat Medicine: From the Korean War to Afghanistan (2019)

11 Kornicki, F., Oral History Testimony Imperial War Museum Sound Archives catalogue reference: 028594

12 Information written and supplied by Richard Kornicki CBE DL, son of
      Franciszek Kornicki and Chairman of the Polish Air Force Memorial
      Committee.

13 Ibid

14 Ibid

15 Ibid

16 Ibid

17 Ibid

18 Ibid

19 Polish Air Force Memorial Committee Official Website.

Airman freed when Americans captured Dulag-Luft near Wetzlar
Germany on 29th March 1945

Picture Credits

Anne Baker 52 and 53

Author collection 27, 44, 132 and 164

Battle of Britain Bunker 30

Richard Kornicki 5, 105, 167, 169 and 172

Exeter Archives 48, 50, 62, 86, 100, 101, 102, 103, 108, 111, 112, 114, 117, 119, 138 and 178

Franklin D Roosevelt Library 76, 77, 83, 88, 94, 97(l), 121, 122, 126, 127, 131, 137, 140, 155, 156, 158 and 190

Jonathan Falconer collection 28, 37, 39 and 129

New York Library Archives 68

Paul Pouwels *(via Wojtek Matusiak)* 149

Polish Air Force Museum RAF Northolt 14, 15, 17, 21, 33, 51, 54, 57, 61 (both), 123, 161, and 170

Rodney Byles 144

Shutterstock 11, 42, 43, 71, 75 and 79

Sikorski Museum 7, 18, 19, 22, 47, 59, 67, 70, 80, 87, 97(r), 106, 107, 124, 142, 145, 146, 147, 150 and 151

Wojtek Matusiak 84, 85, 93, 143 and 152

Index

Y

Yalta Conference 154, 156

Z

Zaremba F/Lt. 79, 80
Zielinski, F/O. 79, 80
Zumbach, J (known as Johnny) 69
Żurakowski, Sqdn/Ldr. 134
Zychowski, A. 96
Zygmunt, W. 96

Acknowledgements

I extend a heartfelt thank you to my friend Rafal Iwo Jarzebski for encouraging me to document the stories of Polish pilots and for providing me with a Polish perspective on historical events. Special thanks are due to Richard Kornicki CBE DL Chairman of the Polish Air Force Memorial Committee for generously sharing his vast expertise. Richard has assisted my research efforts every step of the way and his informative, fascinating tour of RAF Northolt was the highlight of my research journey. In addition to giving me his time and knowledge he read the first chapter drafts, provided essential feedback and supplied original photographs for inclusion in the text. I am extremely grateful for this unequivocal support. I am also deeply indepted to the highly esteemed Wojtek Matusiak for reading and commenting on the final draft. .

I thank Michael Parrott for sharing his historical insights of 307 Squadron, and Rodney Byles for providing operations records, which detail the astonishing story of 300 Squadron's rear gunner, who was flown back to England from France hanging from his Lancaster bomber by only one foot! I am also grateful to the archivists who have assisted my research, especially Steve Clark of the Imperial War Museum; and to Stephen Saunders of ASA productions Ltd for graciously granting me access to the oral history testimony of Franciszek Kornicki. This testimony was recorded during his television series entitled 'Fighting the Blue.' Finally, I thank Ian Bayley for giving me the opportunity to write about the extraordinary, courageous men and women of the Polish Air Force. It has been a humbling experience.